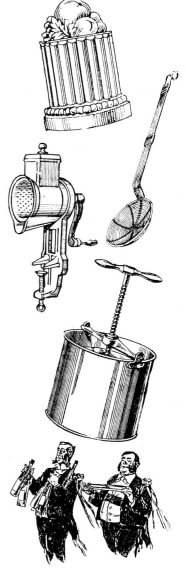

APPETITE FOR CHANGE

Food and Cooking in Twentieth Century Britain
Gill Corbishley

C O N T E N T S

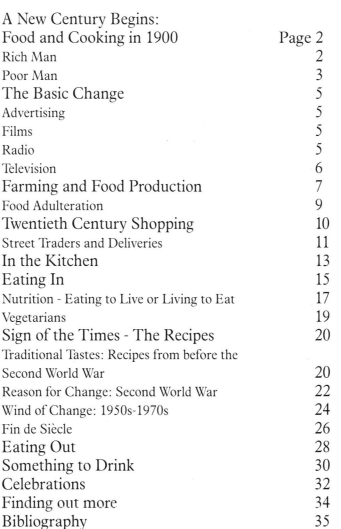

A New Century Begins: Food and Cooking in 1900

Attitudes to food and cooking among British people as the twentieth century began in 1900 varied enormously. "The rich man in his castle, the poor man at his gate" were words from the hymn 'All Things Bright and Beautiful', written only fifty years earlier.

Rich Man

For the aristocrat, the well-to-do landowner or businessman and for most sorts of professional people, food was still exclusively the responsibility of servants. Among the large portion of the population unable to afford servants, the poorer people who lived in the countryside ate better, despite the agricultural depression, than people who lived in towns.

Breakfasts for those who could afford it seem grotesquely large to a generation which considers cereal, eggs and toast excessive. This was the heyday of eggs, bacon, sausages, devilled kidneys, smoked haddock, cold ham and kedgeree. As Margaret Powell writes in 'Below Stairs', " - not one or two of these things but every one." Molly Hughes, in 'A London Home in the 1890s', reinforces this impression with her description of, "a colossal breakfast, including real ham, fish, new-laid eggs, chops and steaks, raspberries and bilberries and bowls of clotted cream at decent intervals on the table," which was served at a Devon hotel.

Since the man of the family was likely to be out at that time of the day, lunch tended to be a less substantial meal. Cold dishes from the night before might be served, or mothers and sisters would eat the midday food cooked for the children. The magazine 'Home Notes' for March 3rd 1894 suggests, for schoolchildren, "Dinner 1 or 1.30 - Meat, potatoes and green vegetables, haricot beans or pease pudding, followed by milk pudding, suet pudding or, occasionally, pastry."

Afternoon tea was a Victorian innovation which proved ideal for entertaining unspecified numbers of

HOME NOTES.

My menu for this week is :—
Mulligatawny Soup.
Salsify Cutlets.
Brazilian Stew.
Calf's Head.
Vanilla Cream.
Cauliflower au Gratin.

friends and acquaintances. Hot toasted teacakes, delicate sandwiches made with cucumber or cress and several sorts of cake served equally for 'At homes', the children's tea and as a stop-gap until dinner was served some time between 8 and 10p.m.

As important as the food which was served at the dinner-table in 1900 was the table's appearance. Mrs Beeton had stressed, in her 'Book of Household Management' in 1861, that even the breakfast table should be decorated with a vase of flowers. At times a Victorian dinner-table, laid with several knives, forks and glasses

Late nineteenth century table setting. By this time it had become fashionable to have a great variety of cutlery and glassware.

English Heritage

for each diner, decorated with an enormous epergne full of fruit, supplied with napkins, jugs and finger-bowls and then draped tastefully with greenery and flowers, seemed to have very little space left for food!

Such elaboration could only be achieved with a large number of helpers. The Census taken in 1891 revealed that 1,549,502 people were employed as servants - 4.9% of the population and 15.8% of the workforce. Dinners consisting of six or seven courses and a choice in each were cooked and handed round the overflowing table by servants, who then ate their own, still substantial, meal 'below stairs'. Margaret Powell writes:

"The amount of food that came into that house seemed absolutely fabulous to me, the amount of food that was eaten and wasted too.... Sometimes with the sirloin they would only eat the undercut and the whole top was left over, so we used to have that for our dinner. Even so, we couldn't eat everything and a lot got thrown away."

But even in January 1894, 'Isobel', the editor of 'Home Notes', felt it necessary to reflect on the problems of keeping servants. She wrote:

"How many people give up housekeeping because the wear and tear of servants is too great for them! Others take flats, so as to decrease the number of servants needed and the consequent worry. The servant question is a difficult problem. How will it end? For the servant class now aspires to something higher, and what

The Smallholder 1913.

MY POULTRY FARM.
The Poultry-Farmer's Weekly Inquire with c
By A. J. SKEY.

is there to take its place?"

Perhaps the readers of 'Home Notes' were not among the richest people in Britain in 1894, but for them the elaborate menu printed opposite in the illustration served as a 'simple and inexpensive menu' for dinner for six to eight people.

A well-equipped kitchen and several servants must have been needed to produce this sort of meal.

PIE WITH CRUST HOLDER.
The GOURMET CRUST-HOLDER AND VENT stands inside any Pie Dish. It supports the Crust and Keeps it Light; Allows Steam to Escape, and Prevents Boiling Over. Made in 2 sizes, 2½ and 5 inches.
Price 6d. each. Post free, 7d.

To be obtained from all Ironmongers, Stores, &c., or

GOURMET & CO.,
MOUNT PLEASANT, LONDON, W.C.

Even relatively working-class people, like Joseph Pearce, who sold beef steak puddings at his London coffee house, reported to the 1891 census that he employed a couple of servants at home, while his own daughter worked as a domestic housekeeper and his 15-year-old son was a waiter.

There were, of course, plenty of jobs for servants to perform. Without labour-saving devices such as vacuum cleaners and washing machines, with no detergents and polishes, probably no gas, electricity or running water, even a small house needed hours of cleaning. Knives were not stainless, silver and brass tarnished easily and cooking utensils of iron, enamel or earthenware became coated with soot on the fire or burned black in the oven.

RIGHT: Joseph Pearce advertising beef steak puddings on sale in his London coffee house in 1891.

Poor Man

Large numbers of working families were not even as well-to-do as Mr. Pearce. All the work involved in providing and cooking their food was done by members of the family, as it is in most families today, but without a single modern convenience! Through the nineteenth century more and more ready-made goods were becoming available in the shops. Tinned fruit, canned meats, ready-made cakes, preserves and sweets were on sale, but such things were too expensive for many people. Seebohm Rowntree made a record of the weekly menu of a working man in York in 1901. The diet

STOP HERE FOR
PEARCE'S
BEEF STEAK
PUDDINGS.
As Nice as Mother Makes Them.
IF YOU DON'T BELIEVE IT ASK ANY WORKING MAN.
6,760 Customers in a Day.

Public Record Office.

of the family consisted almost exclusively of bread, potatoes, pork, eggs, butter, tea and coffee. This lack of variety, as well as the small quantities of food people could afford must have contributed to the 41% of volunteers for the army in the Boer War who were found to be too undernourished to serve.

'The British Workman and Home Monthly Annual' for 1907 illustrates one very common method of saving some of the worker's precious income. Each month's magazine devotes two columns to 'Practical Hints on Poultry for Profit'. Any town family with a back yard was well advised to keep a few hens, to feed themselves and to make a little extra money.

Poor people who lived in the country were also very likely to be able to add to the goods they bought in shops by growing fruit and vegetables, gathering wild foods such as mushrooms and nuts and gleaning from the farmers' fields, as well as securing the occasional rabbit, hare or pheasant. Flora Thompson writes, in 'Lark Rise to Candleford',

"The community was largely self-supporting. Every household grew its own vegetables, produced its new-laid eggs and cured its own bacon. Jams and jellies, wines and pickles, were made at home as a matter of course. Most gardens had a row of beehives. In the houses of the well-to-do there was an abundance of such foods, and even the poor enjoyed a rough plenty."

The accounts of Margaret Dawson, for the first fortnight in June 1907, show the sort of item the poorest housewife had to buy. Her husband earned sixteen shillings a week and this particular bill shows money spent at the drapers, probably on new socks, underwear and overalls. In other weeks there was no chance to save this amount; ten shillings rent had to be paid once a month and because the weather was warm in June it was not necessary to pay for coal.

Although gas cookers were in use by the 1880s and the first electric cookers were manufactured in 1894, at the beginning of the twentieth century most kitchens were dominated by the cast-iron ranges which had been invented a hundred years earlier. They came in varying sizes and the larger, more expensive types could be used simultaneously for boiling, frying and baking. But poor families like those of the Dawsons and Flora Thompson still had only an open grate to cook on. In many parts of the country bread and other dishes for baking were still taken to the communal oven until after the First World War while other meals were made by hanging a saucepan or kettle over the fire- or balancing a frying-pan on the top. The cold meat left on the Sunday joint would feed the family for several days afterwards.

Throughout history people have thought of the times in which they are living as changing - almost invariably into something worse. The nineteenth century had seen enormous developments in industry and empire. People had become so wealthy in such large numbers that they even had time to worry about the squalid and unhealthy lives of the workers in industrial towns. Public Health and Employment Acts had made conditions better by 1900. Publications like 'The British Workman' were full of articles about philanthropists such as Dr. Barnardo and the work of the National Society for the Prevention of Cruelty to Children. Yet the differences of quantity and variety of diet between those who produced 'Home Notes' and 'The British Workman' and those who attempted to feed themselves on a workman's wage in an industrial town were still more pronounced than the difference in diet between rich and poor had ever been.

Socialist idealists such as William Morris blamed industrialisation for the country's condition. The Arts and Crafts movement sought a return to

medieval values, glorifying the healthy, rosy-cheeked country labourer and rejecting machines and factories. But in reality the twentieth century has of course seen industrial and technological change undreamt of by Morris.

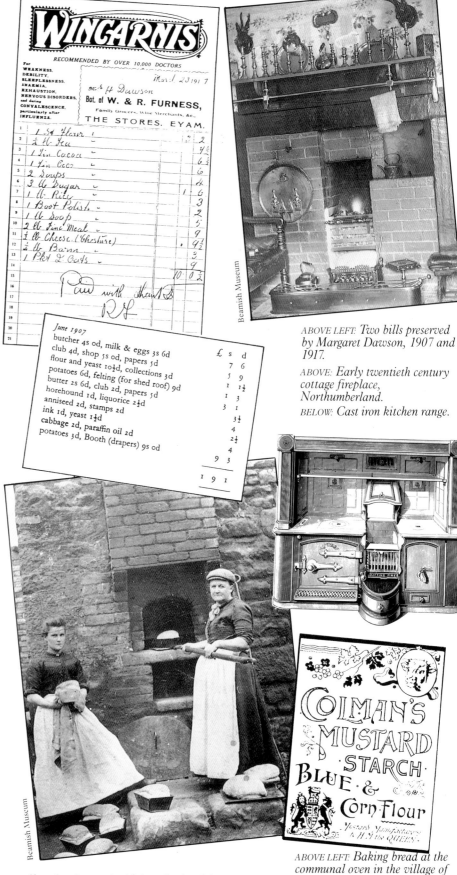

ABOVE LEFT: *Two bills preserved by Margaret Dawson, 1907 and 1917.*

ABOVE: *Early twentieth century cottage fireplace, Northumberland.*

BELOW: *Cast iron kitchen range.*

ABOVE LEFT: *Baking bread at the communal oven in the village of Clara Vale, Northumberland, c1914.*

4

The Basic Change

Comparison of food and cooking for rich and poor in 1900 and comparison in the 1990s demonstrates immediately what have been the major changes during the twentieth century. Today the very poorest families have access to a variety and quantity of food which was inconceivable in 1900. Developments in transport, food production and preservation and communication have all contributed to this.

But perhaps the most striking contrast between 1900 and the 1990s is the way in which the differences between food and cooking in rich households and in poor households have been narrowed. There are still obvious differences caused by lack of money, but instant communication, beginning with radio and films and compounded by advertising and television, has made for far greater uniformity of aspiration and appearance in the kitchen than there was in 1900. Just as blue jeans are worn by both rich and poor, burgers and coke are available to everyone, from royalty to single-parent families supported by government assistance.

Advertising

From the end of the nineteenth century advertisements were making their impact. The 'Liebig Company's Extract of Meat' (renamed 'Oxo' in 1900) showed elegant china and a smartly-dressed cook, while the pictures on posters displayed for Fry's and Terry's chocolates and Peek Frean cakes and biscuits conveyed the message that upper-class and up-to-date people such as the lady cyclist in the Peek Frean advert ate these products. It is interesting that these advertisements have been re-issued in the 1990s as part of the 'nostalgia industry'. Modern advertisements for food items such as bread, butter and cereals exploit that nostalgic feeling.

Films

By 1919 the Women's Institute magazine 'Home and Country' carried an article called 'The Cinema in the Village' in which the writer, Mary C. Horne advocated a cinema in every village as "..an ideal state of things..the inhabitants could.... share in the pleasure of seeing the latest thing in the 'Topical News'". They were also able for the first time to see the dining-tables and kitchens which were normal for people other than their close neighbours.

Radio

In 1927 the British Broadcasting Corporation was established and at the end of that year a book called 'Home, Health and Garden' was published which printed the texts of talks ranging from 'Planning an Ideal Kitchen' to national dishes from the West Indies. As more homes became equipped with a wireless, the broadcasters' messages reached thousands more people than the increasing number of cookery books being published could ever hope to do.

But it was the trauma of the Second World War, from 1939 to 1945, which made 'listening in' a national occupation. Eighteen million people listened every day to Charles Hill 'The Radio Doctor', and learned which foods were good for them and how to

The Robert Opic Collection

The Robert Opic Collection

5

cook them. The German sea blockade and the commandeering of food for the troops and those engaged in war work had created all sorts of shortages. The British government also recognised the need to keep the nation healthy. As a result the public was bombarded with help and guidance, including a daily five-minute radio programme 'Kitchen Front', which was on every morning after the eight o'clock news.

The process begun at the turn of the century with the publication of dozens of magazines such as 'Home Notes', all with regular pages of recipes and advice about the home, was expanding and gathering momentum. Although cookery books had been in circulation in Britain since the middle ages, most people's knowledge of food and cooking had been limited to what they ate and saw in the homes of family and friends. Food was treated in different ways in different parts of the country. During the war, families from Canterbury to Chester, rich and poor, town and country-people were at the mercy of the Ministry of Food and were plied with recipes which used only carrots, potatoes and dried eggs!

Television

If the spread of the wireless between 1927 and the 1950s had led to a narrowing of the difference in attitudes to food and cooking between different sections of the British population, this effect was quite eclipsed by the effect of television.

By 1953, the year in which Elizabeth II was crowned and in which thousands of people bought their first television in order to watch the coronation ceremony, a book called 'Cooking with Harben' by Philip Harben 'The Television Chef', had already been published. From almonds, anchovies and artichokes (globe) to whitebait, Yorkshire pudding and Zabaglione Mr. Harben passed on to his audience an accumulation of cookery ideas and experience. His fame was equalled by that of Fanny and Johnnie Cradock, who were ready with recipe suggestions for the recently-invented 'teenager' in 1970. News magazine programmes such as 'Nationwide' and 'Town and Around' invariably featured

a cookery item during the 1960s and 1970s.

By the 1980s this sprinkle of television advice on food and cooking had become an avalanche. In the 1990s children begin learning to cook with the 'Blue Peter' programme. Adults can continue to learn how and what to cook from programmes such as 'Food and Drink' and 'The Roux Brothers', but there is also constant information, from both the Department of Health and from programmes such as 'Food File', about food production and healthy eating.

There are still elaborate, expensive meals eaten every day in Britain at the end of the twentieth century, just as there were at the beginning of the century. The rich man may still be in his castle. One major difference is that the poor man at his gate is quite likely to be as knowledgeable as he is about the variety and the processes involved in food and cooking.

A Television Meal

Menu Suggestions
Dip-'n'-Dunk Platter
Trevor Blakemore's Stuffed Baked Potatoes
Baked Mushroom Cups (Les Pousses d'Ete)
Stuffed Baked Snails (Les Escargots Bourguignons)
Chickens' Livers Saute
Strawberry, Cherry or Raspberry Tartlets with Orange Cream Sauce
Iced Tomato Juice
Chablis Cup

"If you happen to be the proud possessor of a heated trolley everything hot can be slipped into this with the cold items on the bottom shelf.....When there are great occasions on television like the recent Investiture of Prince Charles, either method enables the cook-hostess as well as everyone else to watch....." 'Fanny Cradock Invites' 1970.

By the 1970s 'TV Dinners' were produced on foil trays by frozen food companies. For those who wished to eat something more palatable, Fanny and Johnnie Cradock had some suggestions.

Farming and Food Production

Darby and Joan club members in Great Oakley, Essex in 1968 recalled farming methods in 1900: "There were 50 men employed at Great Oakley Hall and 21 working horses were kept there. Ploughing was done usually with a horse-drawn plough."

A G Street, in 'Farmer's Glory', written in 1932 comments, "But what a number of names there were in those days (1906); carters, shepherds, dairymen, labourers, a foreman, a groom-gardener, and boys and lads innumerable". In 1932 he found that he was employing only a quarter of the number of men on the same farm. By 1992 the Great Oakley Hall farm was run by two men and a part-timer. Many small farms had been completely submerged by larger concerns during the twentieth century. Most of those which remain are large, fully-mechanised concerns using factory-farming methods.

The final quarter of the nineteenth century had been a difficult time for small farmers, faced with the enclosure of the last vestiges of common land and competition from imports of grain and other food from the Empire. But by 1900 a balance had been achieved and farm-owners and tenant-farmers alike were enjoying a proper Victorian prosperity. Machinery, for drilling corn, hay-making, reaping and binding and threshing, was in use. Steam engines travelled from farm to farm, pulling their ploughs, or their mole-drain layers, from side to side of the fields on cables.

By the outbreak of the First World War in 1914, the country was dependent on imports for one half of all its food. Seventy-five percent of its bread corn was coming from overseas. By 1915 losses of shipping were causing food shortages. It wasn't until 1917 that a Food Production Department was built up throughout the country with County Executive Committees vested with powers to order the ploughing and cultivation of fields.

Some men were provided from the army to work on this extra cultivation. But they had to be augmented with prisoners of war, schoolboys and

ABOVE: *Great Oakley Hall Farm, 1920s and 1930s.*
BELOW: *Threshing in c1900.*

Imperial War Museum.

women from the Land Army.

For a few years after the war, many farmers joined the rest of the population of Britain in enjoying the 'Roaring Twenties'. Hunting, shooting and fishing could be indulged in again. In the summer tennis parties and seaside holidays became the order of the day. Corn prices and wages had been guaranteed by the Corn Production Act of 1917 and by the Agricultural Wages Board. Things began to go wrong when the government repealed the guaranteed price for grain in 1921. Farm and stock prices tumbled and agriculture ceased to be profitable.

Ironically, it was the threat of disaster presented by the Second World War which really revolutionised British farming in the twentieth century. With the experience of shortage during the First World War still a vivid memory, the Government was quick to act. 'Dig for Victory' was the slogan, and the farming population responded magnificently. Nearly six million acres of grassland were ploughed, including Windsor Great Park, which became the largest wheat field in Britain. Crops were grown on the Sussex Downs for the first time since Saxon days. By 1944 food production, in terms of calories, had almost doubled, wheat production had increased by 90% over its pre-war level and vegetable production by almost 50%.

Over half of all manual workers kept either allotments or vegetable gardens. Allotments sprang up in the London parks - even in the moat at the Tower of London! Pig Clubs were started up throughout the country because farmers had turned from animal-farming, which must be supported by imported feed-stuffs which were no longer available, to growing wheat and potatoes.

In 1939 the Government began a system of food rationing which was not completely dispensed with until 1954. Because of the changes in food-production at home and the scarcity of imported food, many things which were eaten everyday were almost unobtainable. Ingenious substitutes were made for the variety of ordinary foods like onions, eggs, cheese, bananas, tomatoes, sausages, meat, fish, cakes, biscuits, chocolate, apples, oranges and lemons. The war brought its own crop of recipes. Today we admire the invention of the wartime cook - though we're usually only tempted to taste the products of those recipes as a novelty!

For farmers this successful concentration on home agriculture was an unqualified success. A Slag and Lime Subsidy and other grants were available so that they could obtain fertilisers and introduce mechanisation. Everything they produced was snapped up in the market. Through the network of the

County War Agricultural Executive Committees every single farm was monitored. The Agricultural Act of 1947, passed by the new Labour Government, was designed to save the farmer from the insecurities of pre-war farming. Since then British farming has been increasingly helped by capital grants, tax concessions and price supports.

But in the second half of the twentieth century the story of food and cooking has become separated from the history of British agriculture. Rural electrification began on a major scale in 1953. Giant 'Eiffel Tower' electric pylons provoked the first murmurings against the visual vandalism of the countryside. Combine harvesters, huge metal grain stores and, from the 1970s, vast cylindrical bales, replaced the heavy horse, the wooden barn and sheaves of corn.

Meanwhile imports of cheap animal-feed from the developing countries were used to produce intensively-reared stock, pigs and poultry but a large proportion of grain for bread manufacture was also still imported. In 1973 Britain's entry into the European Economic Community guaranteed more subsidies for farmers, as prices for products were fixed at the Community's headquarters in Brussels. Food imported from countries outside the Community, such as America, Canada and New

Alan McPherson

ABOVE: *Prairie farming with only the remnants of hedges.*

RIGHT: *Supermarket customers are bombarded with leaflets.*

Zealand was, at the same time, subject to high import duties.

For the first few years after this radical change, the relationship between farmers and the consumer was strained. Post-war expansion, the destruction of hedges and ditches to create 'prairie' fields of corn and the over-enthusiastic use of fertilizer and pesticide, now came in for sharp criticism as food-prices shot up and stories of milk-lakes and butter-mountains circulated.

As the century ends, there has been some tempering of these extremes. Production quotas seem to have decreased the size of the surplus food stocks; farmers are being forced to diversify their crops - even to 'set aside' some land from agriculture. At the same time the Green movement has prompted some farms to return to organic farming, without artificial fertilizers and pesticides, and the worst excesses of intensive pig and chicken-rearing are the subject of constant attack.

Food Adulteration

It seems that a large proportion of the British population at the end of the twentieth century is anxious to see some modification in the trend towards food which is chemically-manipulated, even on the farm. The very processes which, in fifty years, have made chicken an everyday meal, apples available throughout the year and bread ideal for sandwiches, are now rejected and despised by many.

Food adulteration with an eye to profit can be documented from the Middle Ages, when flour was 'extended' by the addition of chalk. The first British Food and Drugs Act was passed in 1860 in order to control additions such as: brick dust to cocoa, vitriol or iron sulphate to beer, copper to green pickles and alum, a mineral-salt whitening agent, to almost all bread. There were still insufficient laws to control the ingredients which were put into the first manufactured foods. Various chemical dyes were used to colour jam, egg powders were made which contained no egg and raspberry juice without a hint of fruit. It was during the Second World War that scientists first began putting back into foods vitamins which the manu-facturing process had removed. Bread, for example, was required to contain specified proportions of iron, vitamin B and nicotinic acid, and these regulations still apply today.

During the 1940s great advances were also made in the development of fertilisers and pesticides to help farmers gain a better yield from their crops. Twenty years later people had realised that DDT (dichloro-diphenyl-trichloroethane) could spread through the food-chain after killing the insects at which it was aimed, threatening even human beings.

It was also in the 1960s that people became wary of 'additives' to food which might be harmful. Monosodium Glutamate, much used in Chinese restaurants, was the first cause of alarm. It was said to cause Kwok's Disease, an allergic reaction. Tests made in 1986 have now cast doubt on this diagnosis. Over the following thirty years scares included: cyclamate sweeteners; nitrates and nitrites used as preservatives in bacon and sausages; saccharin sweeteners; tartrazine colouring and fruit preservatives and waxes.

Perhaps it is not surprising that, by 1992, increasing numbers of people yearn to eat 'natural', unadulterated fruit, eggs and vegetables and meat from animals which have not been fed on and injected with chemicals. Salmonella, to be caught from chickens and eggs, and Bovine Spongiform Encephalopathy (BSE), the disease which destroys cows' brains and makes them 'mad', are just two of the threats offered to people's health by food today.

But it is always difficult to judge the benefits or the damage new processes may cause except with hindsight. There are still many gaps in biochemical knowledge, although it is known that chemicals in many of the 'natural' foods we eat and drink, like oxalic acid in spinach, caffeine in tea and coffee and carotene in egg yolks and carrots can also damage the human body. The enormous increase in choice of food which the century has brought has supplied a whole range of problems which are irrelevant to the starving and undernourished.

Twentieth Century Shopping

ABOVE LEFT: *The main street in St Osyth, Essex in c1900.*
ABOVE RIGHT: *The Castle Restaurant and the Home and Colonial Stores in Clacton, Essex c1900.*

The High Street in even the most backward small town in the 1990s looks very different from the way it looked a hundred years earlier.

The motor car is responsible for a great many of the changes - both directly and indirectly. Roads have been widened and decorated with yellow-lines in many former High Streets to make room for the ubiquitous car, but most shops have also been enlarged and altered out of all recognition to provide selling-space for the enormous range of goods which modern transport now supplies everywhere.

Advances in transport and manufacture of food were well under way by 1900. Canning and freezing were now possible and margarine had been invented in the late 1860s. It was possible to bring goods close to their destination by rail. But a typical street scene would still have shown many age-old features. Shops were small and specialised; the butcher's adorned with hanging carcasses, the grocer's full of anonymous sacks and packages from which tea, sugar, flour and bacon must be taken and weighed out in the correct measure. H G Wells describes a typical street of shops in 'The History of Mr Polly':

"Among other shopkeepers in the High Street there was Chuffles the grocer...

and Tonks, the second grocer... Tonks went bankrupt and was succeeded by a branch of the National Provision Company, with a young manager exactly like a fox, except that he barked. The toy and sweetstuff shop was kept by an old woman of repellent manners, and so was the little fish shop at the end of the street. The Berlin-wool shop having gone bankrupt, became a newspaper shop, then fell to a haberdasher in consumption, and finally to a stationer; the three shops at the end of the street wallowed in and out of insolvency in the hands of a bicycle repairer and dealer, a gramophone dealer, a tobacconist, a sixpenny-halfpenny bazaar keeper, a shoemaker, a greengrocer, and the exploiter of a cinematograph peep-show."

Clearly the retail business was a hazardous one! Many people, as illustrated earlier in this book, bought only essential goods, items which could not be grown or manufactured at home. But things were ready to change.

RIGHT: *Ainslie Brothers' butcher's shop in Clacton, Essex in c1905.*

By 1900 hundreds of foodshops over the whole country were part of multiple-ownership chains. John Sainsbury opened his first shop in Drury Lane in 1869, the Maypole Dairy was founded in 1819 and taken over by the Home and Colonial in 1924. Liptons was established in Glasgow in 1871. By 1900 each of these retailers owned many branches in different parts of the country. The variety of goods which could be offered for sale was increasing all the time, as items such as tinned sardines and salmon, condensed milk and bananas became available. From the early part of the century onwards the development of motor-driven transport meant that shopkeepers were increasingly able to get goods on sale quickly.

With a shop full of goods, the next obvious step was to find methods of selling as much as possible. There was no restriction on shop hours, apart from that on Sunday opening, and for the Sainsbury branch in Kingsland High Street in east London this meant opening at 7.30am every day and closing at 9.15pm from Monday to Thursday, 10.45pm on Fridays and at midnight on Saturdays.

It was a common practice, after closing, for shop sales staff in working class areas to have to return the empty beer tankards left on their counters to the pubs. The beginning of the week was always slack, but then time could be spent making up the blue bags for sugar and weighing and parcelling out goods ready for sale.

It was towards the end of the 1920s that more and more proprietary brands began to come into the shops and Sainsbury branches created separate grocery departments and increased the range of own-label products. At this time there were still 80,000 independent grocers, 20% of which were part of a chain. Now the advertising industry was able to make its mark in food retailing, promoting Kellogg's cornflakes, Quaker oats, Horlicks, Ovaltine, John West salmon and Heinz (57 Varieties) baked beans, among others, throughout the 1930s. Even the lack of supplies during the Second World War was turned to good account, as each manufacturer promised to 'be back' as soon as supplies and rationing allowed.

The founder of another of today's

ABOVE: *Sainsbury's first shop at 173 Drury Lane, London photographed shortly before closure in 1958.*

ABOVE: *Sketch of Sainsbury warehouses used as an advertisement on a paper bag.*

giant supermarket chains, Jack Cohen, was the first shop-owner in Britain to introduce the major change in shopping which was really revolutionary. He launched Tesco self-service stores in 1947. Wages had begun rising sharply after the war, all groceries could now be obtained pre-packaged (although it was still possible to buy them loose as well) and he believed it would be profitable to follow the self-service model introduced in America in the 1930s. For a few years Tesco Stores had little success but in 1950 twenty new stores were bought and converted to supermarkets and business continued to grow until, in the last decade of the century, shops have become so big that they are invariably located in purpose-built retail parks, which are completely outside the town.

Important scientific breakthroughs were, of course, as necessary to the shopping revolution as the motor-car and the power of advertising. Clarence Birdseye set up his first fish freezing plant in New York in 1923. Although it had been possible to transport frozen goods for many years, it was his method of quick-freezing which made the production of frozen fish, peas and, later, thousands of other delicacies, possible. Canned goods have remained a good selling item but the development of foil and film-based packaging materials has meant that an ever-widening range of goods is available for sale in food shops. In 1992 air freight brings chilled exotic fruit and vegetables into every town's supermarket several times a week. The season for eating peas disappeared from the calendar in the 1960s and by the 1990s even strawberries and new potatoes could be produced which were almost indistinguishable from their 'natural' seasonal equivalents.

Street Traders and Deliveries

Although supermarket chains account for a high percentage of all food shopping today, vestiges of the past, as described here by Mayhew at the end of the nineteenth century, still remain in weekly markets, street hot potato, hot dog and ice cream vendors and small specialist shops.

"The pavement and the road are crowded with purchasers and street-sellers. The housewife in her thick shawl, with the market-basket on her arm, walks slowly on, stopping now to look at the stall of caps, and now to cheapen a bunch of greens. Little boys, holding three or four onions in their hands, creep between the people, wriggling their way through every insterstice, and asking for custom in whining tones, as if seeking charity. Then the tumult of the thousand different cries of the eager dealers, all shouting at the top of their voices, at one and the same time, is almost bewildering. 'So-old again', roars one. 'Chestnuts all 'ot, a penny a score,' bawls another. 'An 'aypenny a skin, black-ing', squeaks a boy. 'Buy, buy, buy, buy, bu-u-uy!' cries the butcher....'Twopence a pound grapes'. 'Three a penny Yarmouth bloaters.'....'Penny a lot, fine russets,' calls the apple woman: and so the Babel goes on."

But one aspect of food-retailing which is almost extinct is the delivery-man. In 1900 every town street resounded to the clip-clop of hooves as neat, horse-drawn vans from dairies, butchers and grocers made their way respectfully to every middle-class door. Bread and milk deliveries came daily as a matter of course to almost every household for the first half of the century. As the motor-car came into general use shop-keepers proudly acquired vans and lorries painted with their names and combined an increased delivery-round with the running of the shop. In both the towns and remote country districts, the milkman, the bread-man, the fish-man, the butcher, grocer and the 'oil-man', with paraffin for primus-stoves and oil-lamps, were regular visitors.

Relative affluence, since the 1960s, has spread the motor-car not just to most families but to several members of many families. Everyone is out at work, so who is to take delivery of the bread or fish? The result of these tendencies, combined with the spread of supermarkets, is that even the milkman, the final survivor in most areas by the 1990s, is rapidly disappearing.

TOP: Market in Chapel Street Islington in the 1890s.

MIDDLE: Co-op milkman in the 1930s.

FAR RIGHT: The Muffin Man c1900.

RIGHT: Mobile shop deliveries linger on in Buckminster, Lincolnshire 1992.

12

In the Kitchen

The nostalgia industry has made the picture of a nineteenth century kitchen, dominated by its range in more well-to-do houses and built around table and fireplace in poorer ones, familiar to most people at the end of the twentieth century. By 1900 one in four houses with gas had a cooker, but these were all in towns, of course. Other signs of the approaching revolution were refrigerators, introduced in about 1890. Blocks of ice were kept in an insulated cupboard at the top and cooled food in the other compartments. Labour-saving gadgets included mincers, potato-peelers, apple-corers and knife-sharpeners. The first electric cookers were manufactured with hot-plates made with coiled wires inside which did not last long . In 1900 an electric kettle was made, with its element outside.

It was not until the early 1930s that problems of the means of electrical supply and the means of production were sufficiently overcome to allow the possibility of the mass production of electric kitchen appliances. At the end of the First World War perhaps 6% of rich people's houses were wired for electricity. In 1926 the figure was 18%, in 1938 65% and by 1949 86%, but only 2% of houses in 1948 had a refrigerator. In London in 1942 81% of households cooked on a gas-stove or a gas-ring but in the same year the figure in rural Gloucestershire was only 3%. Throughout the country ownership of electric cookers has risen from 6% of houses in 1936 to 18.6% in 1948, to 30% in 1961 and 46% in 1980. In 1989 the Electricity Council estimated that 58% of homes had a refrigerator, 42% a fridge-freezer and 38% a freezer.

As all these new appliances began to be installed in the majority of kitchens, two themes predominated: the first was the escape from drudgery - labour saving devices! An Electrical Development Association pamphlet issued in 1925 promises

"Indeed, Electricity comes as a timely solution of the servant and other problems, which threatened to disturb that most potent factor in civilisation - THE HOME; Electricity provides the modern housewife with a perfect servant - clean, silent, economical.

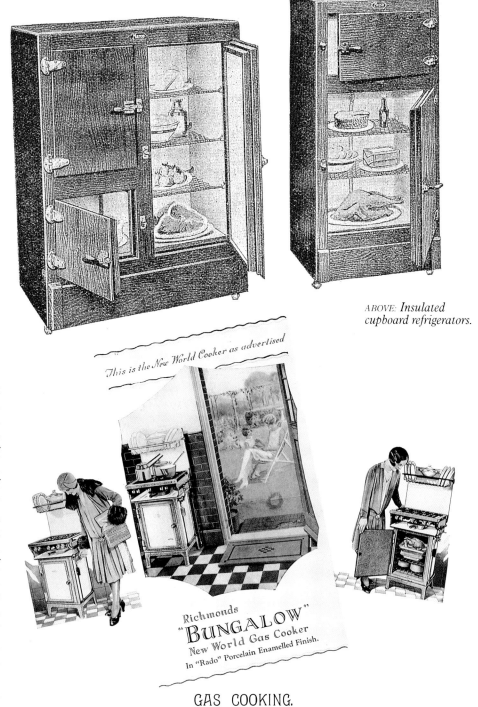

ABOVE: Insulated cupboard refrigerators.

This is the New World Cooker as advertised

Richmonds "BUNGALOW" New World Gas Cooker
In "Rado" Porcelain Enamelled Finish.

GAS COOKING.

PENNY IN THE SLOT COOKERS.

No. O.518.

External Dimensions.			Oven.			Hot Plate.	Burners.	Price.	White Enamelled Crown. Extra.
High.	Wide.	Deep.	High.	Wide.	Deep.				
In cast-iron.									
30 × 18 × 17 in.			19 × 13½ × 11 in.			18 × 17 in.	2	47/6	3/6
As above, but best finish, with polished cornices, hinges, etc.								50/6	3/6

THE IMPROVED GAS ROASTER.
With REMOVABLE White Top and Cast Burners.

No. O.608.

The Roaster is double cased and lined with non-conducting material; the inside is made of specially prepared flexible enamel plates. Hot plate fitted with various sizes of atmospheric burners.

What used to be the labour (hard labour) of hours is now accomplished almost without effort in a matter of minutes"

It is hard to deny that this glowing picture does contain a degree of truth. A survey by the Electrical Association of Women in 1934 found that the jobs of tending to lamps, cooking stoves, fires, washing, ironing and cleaning which took 26 hours per week without electricity were reduced to 7 hours per week with the help of electricity. The fresh-smelling , shiny-surfaced kitchen and instant hot meals which are the norm in late twentieth century Britain are not achieved by hours of brushing, scrubbing and polishing, peeling, chopping, frying and boiling but with electric cleaners, chemical air fresheners and surface sprays and ready-made meals which can be cooked in minutes.

But Hazel Kyrk, whose book 'Economic Problems of the Family' was published in America in 1933 pointed out:

"In household production too, as elsewhere, we have shown a tendency to use the time freed by labor-saving machinery not for more leisure, but for more goods or services of the same general character. The invention of new fuels and cooking equipment (meant) more courses and more elaborately cooked food".

More certainly those inventions freed time for and made possible the second important change in the kitchen during this century - the attempt to produce absolute cleanliness and hygiene.

Early kitchen machinery, used by a tiny minority of rich people's servants, was heavy and cumbersome. The first gas and electric stoves looked like smaller versions of cast-iron ranges and the furniture in kitchens was still wooden or upholstered. Mass production coincided with the Rural Water Supplies Act in 1934, after which two thousand parishes were supplied with piped water within ten years, and with rapid developments in car and aeroplane manufacture. Scientists were also finding more proof of the importance of hygiene to health. The result of all these influences was the ideal of the modern, streamlined, shining white, fully-fitted kitchen.

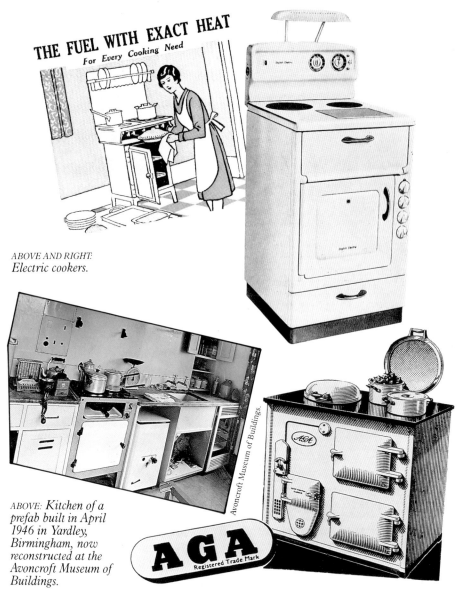

THE FUEL WITH EXACT HEAT
For Every Cooking Need

ABOVE AND RIGHT:
Electric cookers.

Avoncroft Museum of Buildings.

ABOVE: *Kitchen of a prefab built in April 1946 in Yardley, Birmingham, now reconstructed at the Avoncroft Museum of Buildings.*

AGA
Registered Trade Mark

As it became usual for a housewife to manage without servants, fewer courses were cooked and kitchens were organised into separate areas for washing-up, food-storage and eating. Food trolleys and service-hatches were invented to help with some of the problems. Refrigerators meant that perishable foods could be stored for longer and in 1935 the Shelvador refrigerator was the first to be made with shelves in a recessed door. The design is still used today.

Just as the steam engine was superseded by the petrol engine, primus-stoves, which were primed with methylated spirits and burned paraffin, and oil stoves had relatively brief popularity for the first half of the century. They were economical but caught fire very easily and the wicks tended to smoke and smell. Ovens could be operated by this method but they were unreliable for cake and pastry-making.

Another interesting invention was the Aga solid-fuel burner, which was first made in the 1920s in Sweden by Dr Gustav Dalen. Like the old ranges Agas are useful both for heating the house and hot-water supply and for cooking. Agas, and Rayburns, which are usually smaller and were originally made in England by Allied Ironfounders, are still on sale and are often found in use in farms and country house kitchens.

The frozen food industry and therefore the domestic freezer, on the other hand, did not exist until the second half of the twentieth century. Its arrival, the development of the microwave oven from 1968 onwards, and the invention of polythene, tinfoil and clingfilm has made the ideal of a kitchen free from the brutish realities of muddy vegetables and dead animal carcasses quite feasible.

Eating In

What people actually eat can, of course, vary a great deal. Mr Polly, in a book written in 1910 had: "..the cold pork from Sunday and some nice cold potatoes, and Rashdall's Mixed Pickles, of which he was inordinately fond. He had eaten three gherkins, two onions, a small cauliflower head, and several capers with every appearance of appetite, and indeed with avidity; and then there had been cold suet pudding to follow, with treacle, and then a nice bit of cheese. It was the pale, hard sort of cheese he liked; red cheese he declared was indigestible. He had also had three big slices of grayish baker's bread, and had drunk the best part of a jugful of beer..."

In 'Cider with Rosie' Laurie Lee describes large meals prepared in 1918:
"..cauldrons of stew for the insatiate hunger of eight. Stews of all that grew on these rich banks, flavoured with sage, coloured with Oxo and laced with a few bones of lamb. There was, it is true, little meat at those times; sometimes a pound of bare ribs for boiling, or an occasional rabbit dumped at the door by a neighbour. But there was green food of great weight in season, and lentils and bread for ballast. Eight to ten loaves came to the house every day, and they never grew dry. We tore them to pieces with their crusts still warm, and their monotony was brightened by the objects we found in them - string, nails, paper, and once a mouse; for those were days of happy-go-lucky baking. The lentils were cooked in a great pot which also heated the water for the Saturday-night baths."

While in 'The Young Visiters' (sic), published in 1919, Daisy Ashford, aged nine writes:
"A glorious tea then came in on a gold tray two kinds of bread and butter a lovly jam role and lots of sugar cakes. Ethels eyes began to sparkle...."
and:
"Mr. Salteena had a little whiskey to make him feel more at home. Then he eat some curry to the tune of a merry valse...."

Mr Polly was the owner of a small shop, Laurie Lee was a poor child living in a village and Daisy Ashford was a rich child who lived in a town.

What is immediately obvious is that nobody was eating deep-fried foods which had been manufactured and processed before they were bought. By 1900 self-raising flour, yeast and baking powder were available to be bought. Cheese, jelly, custard and blancmange, sauces and pickles, margarine and dried vegetables such as peas and lentils were also being processed in the new 'garden factories'. The magazine 'British Workman and Home Monthly', published in 1906, has glowing articles about the Chivers jam factory, Colmans' mustard factory and Allenbury's baby-milk factory, although other people, like Rose Macauley in 'Non-Combatants and Others', had reservations:
"'..he's a Gordon of Gordon's jams.' 'That sink of iniquity! The girl can have no principle. But jam is going to be nationalised very soon, I trust, like many better things. I hope so.'"
Macaulay in 'Non-Combatants and Others', had reservations.

RIGHT: Chivers Jam Factory, Histon, Cambridgeshire 1906.

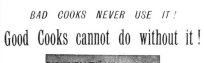

Gill Corbishley.

The Factory in an Orchard.

Porridge had become popular as part of the middle-class breakfast towards the end of the nineteenth century and, by the 1920s, Mr. Kellogg's cornflakes and the Shredded Wheat Company's product from their new factory at Welwyn Garden City were also appearing on breakfast tables. A combination of convenience and advertising has kept cereals continuously popular ever since. Chocolate, which first appeared in its solid form in 1866, has increased in quantity and diversity as people were increasingly able to afford to buy it.

As in most other aspects of British life, the Second World War provides a convenient watershed in the history of twentieth century food. 'Before the War' there were no wrapped, sliced loaves, no sugar-coated cereals, no instant desserts or instant coffee. Rationing ended in 1954 and ten years later those items were all commonplace. The refinement of freezing techniques, followed by 'freeze-drying' and vacuum-sealing coupled with the earnest efforts of importers to obtain exotic raw materials and exotic dishes from all over the world has led to the bewildering choice of menu offered to supermarket shoppers and television viewers today.

The rationing of almost all foodstuffs during the Second World War provides an interesting fixed point for comparison with a modern diet. Amounts allowed varied between 1940 and 1954 but for one week were approximately those listed here:

Milk - 3 pints, Sugar - 225 gm (8 oz), Butter - 50 gm (2 oz), Margarine - 100 gm (4 oz), Cooking fat 85 gm (3 oz), Cheese - 85 gm (3 oz), Bacon - 100 gm (4 oz), Meat - to the value of 1s 2d (2d had to be spent on corned beef), Eggs - 1 (if available) and 1 packet of dried eggs per month, Sweets - 60 gm (2.1 oz), Jam - 50 gm (2 oz), Tea - 50 gm (2 oz).

Another chart comparing quantities of different foods eaten by people between 1950 and 1981 was provided by Christopher Driver in his book 'The British at Table 1940 - 1980' and is also useful for making comparisons.

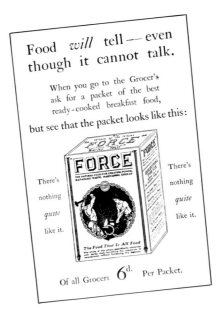

Food *will* tell — even though it cannot talk.

When you go to the Grocer's ask for a packet of the best ready-cooked breakfast food, but see that the packet looks like this:

There's nothing quite like it.

There's nothing quite like it.

FORCE

Of all Grocers 6d. Per Packet.

In their sixty-fifth anniversary magazine published in May 1989, the Good Housekeeping Institute concluded that general food trends during those years showed people eating not so much beef, lamb and fish but more poultry, pork and eggs than they had fifty years previously. They found that less bread was eaten, but more pasta, rice and breakfast cereals; less butter, margarine, lard and whole milk, but more cheese, low-fat and dairy spreads and skimmed milk; fewer potatoes but more vegetables and less sugar and preserves but more alcohol!

	Consumption (ounces per person per week)			
	1950	1960	1974	1981
Liquid milk (pints)	4.78	4.84	4.74	4.01
Other milk (equiv. pints)	0.43	0.31	0.35	0.42
Cheese	2.54	3.04	3.74	3.89
Butter	4.56	5.68	5.61	5.69
Margarine	3.94	3.66	2.60	4.11
Lard and compound cooking fat	3.11	2.63	1.82	1.80
Eggs (number)	3.46	4.36	4.09	3.68
Preserve (inc. syrup, treacle)	6.30	3.21	2.47	2.08
Sugar	10.13	17.76	13.03	11.08
Beef and veal	8.06	8.74	7.41	6.96
Mutton and lamb	5.43	6.63	4.11	4.25
Pork	0.30	2.02	3.20	3.82
Bacon and ham (inc. cooked)	4.52	5.32	4.18	5.17
Poultry	0.35	1.68	5.18	7.30
Sausages	4.01	3.52	3.50	3.41
Other meat products	7.82	7.98	7.57	6.84
Fish, fresh and processed	6.18	4.69	2.76	2.81
Canned fish	0.44	0.95	0.60	0.69
Frozen fish and fish products	n.k.	0.29	0.96	1.42
Fresh green vegetables	13.81	15.34	12.70	11.98
Other fresh vegetables	11.38	9.13	10.20	11.83
Tomatoes, fresh	4.78	4.75	3.74	3.92
Frozen vegetables	n.k.	0.63	2.66	4.88
Canned vegetables	4.55	6.21	7.28	8.00
Potatoes (excl. processed)	62.04	56.14	45.66	38.91
Fruit, fresh	14.41	18.16	17.79	19.97
Canned fruit	3.68	6.84	4.90	2.61
Flour	7.25	6.76	5.30	5.96
White bread	50.91	36.63	28.24	21.85
Brown bread (inc. wholewheat and wholemeal)	2.55	3.35	2.64	5.56
Other bread	4.29	5.49	2.62	3.84
Buns, biscuits, cakes	10.37	11.98	10.08	9.16
Breakfast cereals	1.40	1.80	2.88	3.53
Tea	2.16	2.80	2.24	1.98
Coffee (inc. instant)	0.21	0.39	0.51	0.52
Soups	1.31	2.10	3.46	3.10

Nutrition - Eating to Live or Living to Eat

Although previous generations had known that food is essential to life, it was not until the very beginning of the twentieth century that scientists discovered that certain foods, and certain parts of food, such as the outer covering of rice and wheatgerm in bread, contained elements necessary to keep people healthy.

After doctors had realised, during the Boer War and the First World War, that almost half the male population called up to enlist in the army were not in good enough health to serve, efforts were made during the 1930s to redress the balance. The School Medical Officer for Glossop designed a free school meal to supply children suffering from malnutrition with elements missing from their home food. The Glossop Health Sandwich consisted of:

85 gm (3 oz) of wholemeal bread
21 gm ($\frac{3}{4}$ oz) butter or vitaminized margarine
21 gm ($\frac{3}{4}$ oz) salad; mustard and cress, or watercress, or lettuce or tomato or carrot
42.5 gm ($1\frac{1}{2}$ oz) cheese, or salmon, or herring, or sardine or liver
6 gm ($\frac{3}{16}$ oz) dried brewers' yeast
1 pint of milk and 1 orange, when obtainable; if no fruit 7 gm ($\frac{1}{4}$ oz) chopped parsley is included in the sandwich filling.

By the time the Second World War began, the nation's health, both on the battlefield and at home, had become a Government priority. 'Food Values in Wartime' by Violet G Plimmer was one of several books which sought to educate the public. She wrote:
"The ordinary pre-war diet was not wholesome. It contains too many unwholesome foods, such as white bread, sugar, fats of low vitamin value, vegetables overcooked or wrongly cooked. To restore its wholesomeness such a diet required many additions."

Rationing provided a good opportunity to redistribute vital foodstuffs, like milk, eggs and orange-juice, to the fighting men, mothers and babies who needed them most.

As shortages became a memory and

GROWING UP
and building up

The 'teen age is a critical stage of development. The young people are still growing. Longer hours and the harder condit.ons of business, compared with school, are a further tax. Right feeding is most important at this time.

There is a helpful booklet, just published, called " How to plan meals for children from 12 to 17 years of age." Why not send a post-card for it to the Ministry of Food, Food Advice Division, London, W.1 ?

Meantime, here are some pointers for you :

Breakfast
Always give some builder (milk, or dried eggs, or fish, fresh or canned) and some energiser (porridge, fried potatoes or bread). Rushing out on an empty stomach is bad for everyone; especially for growing youngsters.

Mid-day Meal
Impress upon young workers the need for them to have a real good meal, *including greens or a salad,* at mid-day. If they cannot come home, persuade them to go to their canteen or a British Restaurant if there's one near them. Buns and tea are all very well for ' elevenses ' or tea-time, but *not* for the mid-day meal. If you put up packed meals, remember that each meal should include : (1) a builder; (2) a protector, such as fruit, when you can get it, a raw vegetable salad in a container, or salad sand-wiches; (3) energy food, which generally looks after itself in bread, pastry, turnover, cake, etc.

► HERE IS A SUGGESTION FOR ◄
► ONE PACKED MEAL ◄

Turnover filled with sausage meat, cooked dried peas, herbs, parsley, and chopped leek or onion. Raw cabbage salad in a screw-top jar. Oatmeal scones and jam.

Evening Meal
Here again, try to get in a builder, a protector, and an energiser. For example, an omelette or scrambled eggs, made with dried eggs is a first-class builder. Add some lightly cooked green vegetables or a salad — some watercress or mustard and cress is excellent — and some fried potatoes or bread and margarine and you have a perfect meal. So easy to prepare, too, and a boon if you have to return from your own work to cook. *For a bed-time drink,* try soup sometimes for a change.

EXTRAS FOR THE UP TO 18's

Young people up to 18 are entitled to half a pint of milk a day. Up to this age, too, they should be able to get National Milk Cocoa where they work at a price of not more than 1d. per cup. If they're not getting it, urge them to ask about it. Milk and National Milk Cocoa are valuable building foods. Please do your best to make sure that your young people have their full share of them. (S88)

ISSUED BY THE [MF] MINISTRY OF FOOD

the country moved into the 'Swinging Sixties', the concept of eating for health ceased to be quite so mainstream. Coffee-Bars were booming (the first espresso coffee machine was imported in 1952) and self-service restaurants selling fried food were springing up all over the country. Two minorities remained obsessed with the content of the food they ate - the slimmers and those who chose to live an 'alternative' life in communes, often guided by a 'guru' from an Eastern country and eating food such as brown rice, lentils and vegetables.

Thirty years later both these attitudes have become preoccupations for many thousands of people. There are no longer many people living in communes but a survey of 2,000 consumers by the Independent newspaper in 1986 reflected a strong interest in 'healthy eating'. 63% of the people interviewed said they had increased their fruit and vegetable intake, many had changed from white

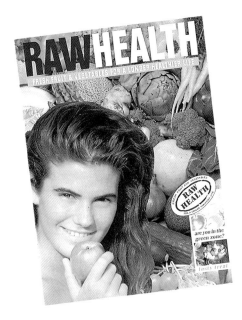

bread to brown, 33% said they were eating more fish and most said they were eating more fibre and less meat. Strangely, market statistics recorded at the same time showed that fruit and vegetable consumption had actually fallen in the previous five years and that the nation was eating more meat per head than it had done ten years earlier!

"An apple a day keeps the doctor away" is still an acknowledged truth at the end of the twentieth century, but children are far more likely to eat a daily packet of crisps than to eat a daily apple. Crisps were invented in France by a M. Cartier. He came to England and his business was bought, in 1919, by Frank Smith, who then developed Smith's Crisps. Until the 1960s crisps were packed in waxed paper and stayed crisp for only one day. The invention of superior packaging has allowed the industry to reach its present size.

Nevertheless, in the 1990s, however unwholesome the food we actually do eat may be, the British nation has information constantly presented to it about the advisability, and the virtue, of eating with discretion in order to remain slim and healthy. Particular elements in foods have been blamed for causing the diseases of civilisation, cancers, thrombosis and heart disease. The 1991 World Health Organisation report on Diet, Nutrition and Chronic Disease was quoted by Colin Spencer in an article in 'The Guardian' on April 4th 1992. He writes:

"The range of convenience foods is indeed huge, but when you analyse the ingredients they tend to be the same: refined flour and sugar, saturated fats and salt; the food is given colour and taste by chemical additives; what protein there is derives often from carcass off-cuts and MRM (mechanically recovered meat), which need not be disclosed on the label. According to the WHO report, this is food 'characterised by an excess of energy-dense foods rich in fat and free sugars', deficient in complex carbohydrates and linked with the emergence of a range of chronic non-infectious diseases, particularly coronary heart disease and various cancers."

On the other hand, the responsible American Food and Drug Administration (FDA) carried out a very thorough study of sugar in 1986 and concluded that its only danger was in its contribution to tooth decay. An FDA official announced,

"We can now state categorically that there is no evidence at all to link sugar with obesity, diabetes, high blood pressure, hyperactivity or heart disease."

It might be argued that both healthy food and slimming are more useful today to manufacturers and advertisers as a means of selling more food that they are to the British public as a whole.

Meanwhile a Gallup Poll to discover the Briton's perfect meal found, in 1947, that it was tomato soup, sole, roast chicken with roast potatoes, peas and sprouts, trifle and cream, cheese and biscuits, coffee and wine. And in 1986? The answer to the same question was vegetable soup, prawn cocktail, steak with chips, peas, carrots and salad, gateau, cheese and biscuits, coffee and wine.

"Frederica realised she would have to go shopping. The spam had not done, really, once, and would certainly not do again. She realised she had never cooked dinner for anyone, and didn't really know how. She realised she had almost no money. It was before the days of Elizabeth David and her ideas of what constituted a nice dinner for two were derived from 'Woman's Own' and her mother's exceedingly infrequent practical example. Grapefruit with cherries in, and a roast duck, and fresh fruit salad with cream? Hors d'oevre and steak with jacket potatoes and salad, followed by baked bananas with rum and cream? Ice cream? Soup with hot rolls followed by trout followed by trifle with lots of sherry in it?"

'The Virgin in the Garden' A S Byatt 1978.

Vegetarians

A preoccupation with eating only food which would promote good health was not simply an invention of the 1960s. In 'Non-Combatants and Others' by Rose Macaulay, published in 1916, one can read,

"Daphne was willing her to health and happiness, trying, in fact, suggestion. Daphne believed in health suggestion, as well as health food. She belonged to societies for promoting both. She had often in the past made health suggestions to Alix, but Alix had not always taken them."

In the first years of the century Socialism and vegetarianism, exemplified by giants such as George Bernard Shaw, seemed to go naturally together. 'Simple Vegetarian Cookery' by Dr Paul Carton, published in 1931 states:

"It is not essential to health to eat meat at every meal, or even every day. The hardy peasants of earlier times took very little, confining themselves to the produce of their own poultry yards. It is possible to keep in good health without eating any meat. Whole nations at the present day - the Hindus, for instance- abstain from it. Vegetarians exist in great numbers, and show remarkable physical resistance."

It was the Cranks restaurant, which opened in London in June 1961, which set the style for the next two decades of vegetarianism. A recipe book soon followed and many people were enthusiastic about wholewheat, 'no-knead' bread instead of white, sliced and meals like Homity Pie, Buckwheat Bake and Lentil and Cheese Wedges. The news of the imminent closure of the original Cranks restaurant at the end of February 1992, provoked a chorus of general agreement in the press that the comparative heaviness of this sort of food had been superseded by restaurants which served and recipe-books which promoted varied delights such as rocket salad, grilled vegetables, olive-oil bread and mozzarella cheese. In fact a management buy-out has kept the restaurant open.

It is easy to add other, newly-popular, foods to the list above: pasta, courgettes, peppers, aubergines, avocado pears, garlic, pitta bread,

yoghurt and fromage frais, for instance. They demonstrate that the change in people's food since 1900 is not only caused by the variety of processed and ready-to-eat foods now available. A list compiled by Christopher Driver for an article in 'The Guardian' on March 11th 1992 suggests almost 100 national food products and recipes which could now be considered to be in danger of becoming extinct.

Signs of the Times - The Recipes

Traditional Tastes: Recipes from before the Second World War

Sheep's Head Soup

This is a nourishing soup, and the head itself can be served afterwards for the meat course. Clean the head and chop it in half, take out the brains; the end of the nostril should be chopped away altogether, on account of the mucus. Place the head in three quarts of cold water, with a little salt, 12 leeks cut in small pieces, and a little carrot and turnip; when it has gently simmered three hours remove the meat and keep it hot. Thicken the soup with 3 ozs of fine Florador*, previously wetted with a little milk or water; this should be boiled in the soup, from fifteen to twenty minutes; it is then ready for serving. The scum which rises during the preparation must be carefully removed with a wooden spoon; no straining is required. If desired clear, omit the Florador. To serve the head, make a nice thick parsley or sharp sauce, and pour over it in the dish. The brains should be boiled separately tied up in muslin, and placed in boiling water; they will take about twenty minutes to cook, and should then be chopped with a leaf or two of sage, and some pepper and salt. Serve on a separate dish, with the sheep's tongue in the middle.

* use plain flour

'Middle-Class Cookery' Vera c1900.

Brown Bread Soup

Boil any stale brown bread to a jelly with water and a little milk, adding an onion or celery, if liked. When the bread is nearly transparent, add enough milk to make it creamy, a small bit of butter, pepper, and salt. Serve very hot with fried bread. This soup is popular with our Continental friends, and ought to be more widely known in England.

'Home Notes' Isobel 1894.

Tasty And Cheap

1 Fresh Haddock (about 2lb)	biscuits, cream crackers, or thin lunch pounded into crumbs
3 fresh herrings	4 or 5 spring onions
2 eggs	small sprig of parsley
1 small teacup of breadcrumbs, or broken pieces of any dry	saltspoonful of salt
	shake of pepper

Have the large bone taken out of the fish, and as many of the small ones as possible. Have the fish thoroughly clean, and cut into convenient pieces, and put all through the mincer. Chop the onion and parsley finely, and add to minced fish; add salt and pepper, now add 1 egg and white of the other, and mix all together very thoroughly with a wooden spoon, and make the mixture into balls about the size of an egg.

Have some boiling water ready and put the fish balls in, with just enough water to cover the fish. Sprinkle a little salt and pepper over, and allow to boil 30 minutes. Take off the gas and allow to cool. Now beat the remaining yolk of egg, and add to contents of saucepan, put over gas for a few minutes to thicken the gravy. This dish can be eaten hot with boiled potatoes for dinner, or is delicious when cold.

'Daily Express Prize Recipes For Fish Cookery' c1925.

Rolled Veal

A loin of breast of veal,
one pound of bacon, veal
stuffing, seasoning, stock.

Method: Bone a loin or breast of veal, and stuff it with veal forcemeat made with bacon, breadcrumbs, and eggs, and flavoured with lemon peel, sweet herbs, nutmeg, salt and pepper. Tie it up tightly in a cloth, keeping it in the shape of a large sausage, and stew gently for four hours in some well-flavoured stock. Let it cool a little, take off the cloth and tighten it round the roll, then put it under heavy weights till quite cold. Glaze it, and garnish the dish with small pieces of savoury jelly.

'Home Notes' Isobel 1894.

Rissoles of Game

½lb any cold game	½lb shortcrust pastry
4oz cooked ham or bacon	1 egg beaten
one truffle cut in dice	breadcrumbs or vermicelli
6 mushrooms	salt
5 or 6 tbsps of sauce or thick gravy	pepper.

Method: Remove all skin and bone, chop meat and ham finely and add mushrooms and truffle. Add enough sauce to moisten, shape into balls the size of large chestnuts. Roll out pastry thinly. Cut out circles.
Lay a ball of mixture on each round of pastry. Brush round edges with a little cold water, fold one half over the other and press edges together. Brush each one with beaten egg. Cover with breadcrumbs or vermicelli, broken small.
Fry each one in hot fat until golden brown.
Mrs J M Pile, Great Oakley 1911.

To Cook Cauliflower, Brocoli*, Cabbage, Brussels Sprouts, Savoys, and Lettuces.

They should be washed well, and allowed to remain in cold water, with a little salt, an hour or so before cooking. The salt helps to draw out the insects, etc. The outside leaves should be removed and the thick stalks cut crossways. Put the vegetables into boiling water, allowing half an ounce of salt to two quarts of water, and boil gently, with the lid off the saucepan, until tender.
Cauliflower should be placed in the saucepan with the head downwards, and when served white sauce should be poured over.
* This is the original spelling.
'Domestic and Economical Cookery Recipes' Lillie Richmond 1892.

—— Some Everyday Puddings ——

Fig Pudding

Half a pound of dried figs (sliced)	a quarter of a pound of flour
a quarter of a pound of moist sugar	a pinch of salt
six ounces of chopped suet	a saltspoonful of grated nutmeg
a quarter of a pound of fine white breadcrumbs	two beaten eggs and half a gill of milk.

Mix the dry ingredients thoroughly, then moisten with the eggs and milk; pour into a buttered basin, tie down with a pudding cloth, and boil for two hours and a half.
'The Smallholder' Magazine 1913.

*Battenburg Cake

Foundations:

6ozs margerine	Almond Paste:
6ozs sugar	5ozs ground almonds
6ozs flour	5ozs icing sugar
3 eggs	5ozs castor sugar
Little lemon rind	Flavouring
½ teaspoonful baking powder	1 egg (about)
Carmine	Jam, butter icing or royal icing

Cream the butter and sugar, add beaten egg slowly; sift in flour and baking-powder, add lemon rind; mix well. Put half the mixture into flat dripping-tin, colour the other half pink, and bake in a similar tin. Bake in moderate oven about 30 minutes; when cold; cut into strips about 1½ inches square. Spread the outside of each strip with jam, place a white and pink one, then on top a pink and white strip. Roll out almond paste, wrap neatly round the four strips, make even sides, trim the ends, decorate top with coloured icing royal icing.
Method: for Almond Paste: Mix almonds, sieved icing sugar, and castor sugar, add flavouring top the eggs, mix all to a very stiff paste.
*Battenburg was the original name of the Mountbatten family.
'Manual of Modern Cooking' Lindsay and Mottram 1927.

Boston Cream

The whites of two eggs	one ounce of tartaric acid
one pound of lump sugar	six drops of essence of
one quart of cold water	lemon.

Put the sugar and water into a pan, boil fast for half an hour. Strain through fine muslin. Allow it to stand until cold, and then add the acid crushed to powder and essence of lemon. Beat the whites to a stiff froth on a plate, and stir well together until all is dissolved. Pour into bottles. Will keep two or three months.

To make a drink: Put two large tablespoonfuls into a glass, fill to within an inch of the top with cold water, stir in as much carbonate of soda as will lie on a sixpence; it is ready for drinking when it froths up to the top.
'The Smallholder' Magazine 1913.

Liquid Milk

To prepare liquid milk - from dried milk

3 tablesps. (2oz) Dried Milk
2 breakfastcups water

Method: Mix the dried milk with 2 tablespoons of the water and beat very hard with a wooden spoon or a whisk until smooth. Add the rest of the water gradually and stir or whisk well.

Two Minute Soup

4 Tablesp. Dried Milk	Extract or
2 Breakfastcups Cold Water	2 Tablesp. chopped Parsley or Pinch of salt
1 Teasp. Vegetable or Meat	

Method: Mix milk as above. Bring to boil and stir in the extract or parsley and salt.
'Food from Overseas' HMSO 1941

Cod Pancakes

½lb salt cod cooked and flaked in small pieces	Batter
	4oz flour
1 level tablespoon chopped parsley	1 level tablespoon dried egg (dry)
Salt and pepper	2 level teaspoons baking powder
2 level tablespoons mixed herbs	Salt
6oz mashed carrots	½lb pint water
	(Makes four helpings)

Make the batter by mixing together all the dry ingredients, adding sufficient water to make a stiff batter. Beat well and add the remainder of the water. Add to the batter the flaked cod, parsley, seasoning, herbs and carrots. Melt some fat in a pan and when smoking hot drop in large spoonfuls of mixture. Brown the pancakes on one side then turn over and brown the other.
Ministry of Food Pamphlet

Corned Beef Pie

3 rations of corned beef (6d worth)	1 teaspoonful chopped parsley
1 cup of finely shredded raw vegetables (carrot, potato, leek, swede, etc)	Small piece fat
	Short crust pastry (6ozs flour, 3ozs fat)
1 oxo cube	1 dessertspoon flour

Melt the fat in a small pan and lightly fry the vegetable. Stir in the flour and cook a few minutes. Add 1 cup of cold water and the crumbled Oxo cube. Stir until thickened. Draw off the heat, add cubed meat, parsley and seasoning to taste. Line a small plate with pastry and spread it with the meat mixture. Cover with pastry, seal the edges and decorate with pastry leaves. Bake in a moderate oven 30 minutes.
Oxo advertisement 1942.

'Lord Woolton Pie'

——— 5-6 persons ———

'Take 1lb each of diced potatoes, cauliflower, swedes and carrots, three or four spring onions, if possible one teaspoonful of vegetable extract and one tablespoonful of oatmeal. Cook all together for 10 minutes, with just enough water to cover. Stir occasionally to prevent the mixture from sticking. Allow to cool; put into a pie dish, sprinkle with chopped parsley, and cover with a crust of potatoes or wholemeal pastry. Bake in a moderate oven until the pastry is nicely brown and serve hot with brown gravy.
Ministry of Food Pamphlet.

Let the Hay-box cook for you. Stews, soups, haricot beans, porridge or root vegetables will cook by themselves in a hay-box. Allow at least twice as long as for ordinary simmering. If necessary, food can be left to cook in the box all day or all night. The secret of success in hay-box cookery is to put the food into the box *boiling* hot and to "hot up" before serving.

Orange Flavour Whip

1lb stewed or bottled
    plums
2½ level tablespoons
    dried milk

3 level tablespoons of the
    new sweet marmalade

Strain the plums and keep the juice for a sauce or jelly. Mash the plums and mix with the milk and marmalade. Beat well. Serve in individual dishes topped with marmalade or custard.

Other delicious combinations are apples and plum jam; rhubarb and raspberry jam - and you think of many others. When you use a somewhat colourless fruit it is best to combine it with a red one.
These fruit whips are very easy to make and are favourites at children's parties.
Ministry of Food Pamphlet 1945.

Drying of Fruit, Vegetables and Herbs

Drying is an economical method of preserving, as the cost of equipment is small. All that is required is a number of trays made to fit into an oven or any available warm place, such as a drying cupboard.
Some fruits, such as apples, grapes, pears and stone fruits, are suitable for drying, but small fruits and berries do not generally give satisfactory results.
The most suitable vegetables for drying are beans and peas. Leafy and root vegetables may be dried, but they are better used in the fresh state wherever possible.
'Preserves from the Garden' Ministry of Agriculture and Fisheries 1940.

Plain Wheatmeal Cake

4 tablesp. N.W. Flour
4 tablesp. White Flour
1½ tablesp. Sugar
1½ tablesp. Chopped
Dates or any other Dried
    Fruit
1 teasp. Spice

1 tablesp. Dried Milk
1 Medium Carrot (grated)
1 tablesp. Dripping,
    Cooking Fat or Margarine
1 tablesp. Treacle or Syrup
1½ teasp. Baking Powder
Salt

Method: Rub the fat into the flour. Add the rest of the ingredients and mix to a dropping consistency with water. Put into a greased or lined baking tin and bake in a moderate oven for 1½ to 2 hours.
'Food from Overseas' HMSO 1941.

Cocoa with Dried Milk

3 tablesp. Dried Milk

2 Breakfastcups
    Water Cocoa Powder

Method: Mix the milk powder with the cocoa powder; stir in the boiling water gradually; boil one minute.
'Food from Overseas' HMSO 1941.

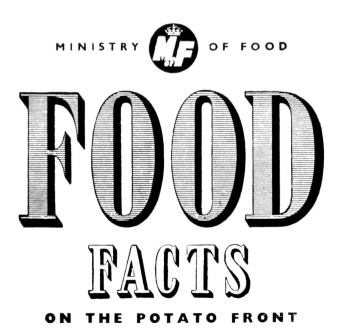

MINISTRY **MF** OF FOOD

FOOD FACTS

ON THE POTATO FRONT

French Onion Soup

Quantities for six people:

2 tablespoons butter	2 pints good beef stock
2 tablespoons oil	½ pint dry white wine
1½ lb onions, thinly sliced	6 slices French bread
2 cloves of garlic, crushed	8oz grated Gruyere cheese
½ teaspoon granulated sugar	Salt and freshly milled black pepper

Heat the butter and oil together in a large saucepan. Stir in the sliced onions, garlic and sugar and cook over a fairly low heat for about 30 minutes, or until the base of the pan is covered with a nutty brown, caramelized film (this browning process is important as it helps the colour of the resulting soup, and also helps considerably with the flavour). Now pour on the stock and wine, bring the soup to the boil, cover and simmer gently for about an hour.

Then taste and season the soup with salt and freshly milled black pepper (and if you really need a stomach-warmer add a tablespoon or two of brandy). Now toast the slices of French bread and spread them with butter. Place each slice in a fireproof soup bowl, ladle

the soup on top, and when the toast surfaces sprinkle grated Gruyere cheese over the surface of each bowl. Grill until golden brown and bubbling.

'The Evening Standard Cook Book' Delia Smith 1978.

Shellfish and Grapefruit Salad

This sounds an unusual combination, but when prepared it is a real palate tickler.

1 pint picked prawns or other shellfish	lettuce and tomato for salad
1 grapefruit	French dressing as required
1/4 cucumber	

Method: Prepare the lettuce and arrange in a salad bowl with the tomatoes. Peel grapefruit removing pith, pips, and skin from the segments and put into a bowl with the juice. Peel the cucumber and cut into dice. Add cucumber and shellfish to the grapefruit, and stir in gently sufficient dressing.

Pile the mixture into the centre of the salad bowl, and garnish with·a few prawns. Serve at once.

'Town and Around Recipes' Zena Skinner 1965.

Duck in Orange Sauce

——— 4-6 servings ———

A duck, unless specially fattened for the table, is usually·a disappointing bird to carve; the yield is markedly less than from a chicken of the same weight. This recipe is designed to make the bird go further by enrobing it in a sauce that is rich and luscious. The result is a somewhat sumptuous dish, not to be attempted by those who prefer austerity.

1 duck; a wild duck would do particularly well in this recipe	1 large carrot
	2 bay leaves
	1 tablespoon flour
2 oranges, or other citrus fruits in this order of preference: Seville oranges, grapefruit (1 enough), sweet oranges, lemons, tangerines (4 would be needed);	4oz mushrooms (omit if unprocurable), 1 glass (4 oz). port or sherry - Empire wine will do admirably, or, failing that, use 1 pint of rough cider in a manner to be described later.
1 large onion	

Method: Two hours before dinner put the trussed duck in a slow oven (gas oven mark 2 or C; electric, 300 F.) Do not put it in a baking tin of fat, but let it stand on the grid shelf with a baking tin on the shelf below to catch the fat that will drip from the bird in liberal measure. Put the giblets on to boil with half the onion, half the carrot, the bay leaves, the juice and rinds of the oranges, water to cover. If you are unable to use port or sherry, let the covering liquid be 1 pint cider made up to quantity with water. Cook this stock gently for 1 hour. Strain, and make up (or reduce by rapid boiling in an open pan) the liquid to 1 pint. If you have a pressure cooker you can make the stock in a quicker and simpler way; put the giblets, etc, in the pressure cooker with exactly 1 pint water (or cider, if that is what you are using) for 15 minutes. About 1 hour before dinner start making the sauce. Chop the remaining onion and carrot as finely as possible. Into a heavy saucepan, or a frying pan if you are more used to working that way, measure not more than 2oz of the fat that has dripped from the duck - there should be plenty by now. make this fat hot in the pan and in it fry the finely chopped onion and carrot until they are browned. Stir in the 1 oz of flour and cook till that too begins to brown. Now add the stock gradually, stirring well, and bring it up to boiling point so that it thickens. Add the wine and the stalks of the mushrooms; simmer for 10 minutes. Adjust the seasoning and colour the sauce with gravy browning if it looks pale.

About ½ hour before dinner remove the baking tin from the oven and from it drain every particle of fat - a most valuable bonus. Put the duck - nearly cooked by now - into the empty tin and pour the sauce right over it, see that it is all covered. Lay the mushroom tops, whole and washed, but not peeled, along the breast of the bird in a neat and decorative manner. Put it into the oven for another half hour's cooking. Soon the coating sauce will dry on the bird: spoon some more sauce over it to give it a fresh coat. Repeat this several times. Ten minutes before time, put the duck into a dish fit for the table, and put it into the lowest part of the oven to keep it hot. Pour the sauce from the baking tin through a strainer into a cold basin. Let it stand for 5 minutes, then skim off the top layer to remove all fat. (Set this aside for clarifying later - another little bonus.) Return the sauce to the saucepan and re-heat, beating well to work in any fat there may still be, and send it to the table separately in a sauce boat.

Although it has taken some time to give this recipe in detail (many of the instructions will be superfluous to advanced cooks), it is really not at all difficult. The achieving of it will give you great satisfaction, and the eating of it will give you a passing glimpse of that better time which still seems so far away.

'Cooking with Harben' Philip Harben 1953.

Petits Pois à la Française

For four people:	6 lettuce leaves
2lb young peas, freshly shelled	8 spring onions
	2oz onions

Trim the onions, as you only need the bulbous white part (save the green bits for salads). Break the lettuce leaves into wide strips, then melt the butter in a thick-based saucepan. Add the onions, lettuce and peas, stir well, then add 4 tablespoons water, a pinch of sugar and 1 level teaspoon salt.

Bring to simmering point, then cover the saucepan and let it cook over a very gentle heat for 25 to 30 minutes, but keep an eye on it and shake the pan now and then to prevent the vegetables sticking (and add just a little more water if you think it needs it).

These are delicious served with chops or steaks and buttered new potatoes.

'The Evening Standard Cook Book' Delia Smith 1978.

Lemon Sponge Gateau

(no cooking)

8 sponge cakes	3 eggs separated
4oz best margarine or butter	2 large or 3 small lemons
6oz caster sugar	small carton $\frac{1}{4}$pt double cream (optional)

Split sponge cakes and line 6 inch cake tin (with loose bottom).

Cream fat and sugar, add yolks of eggs and beat well, stir in rind and juice of lemons. Beat whites till stiff and fold into mixture. Pour into tin and cover top with remaining sponge cakes. Gently press plate on top and weigh down. Leave in fridge for approx. 24 hours. Turn out and coat with cream (whipped). Decorate if desired.

Grange Park Women's Institute Recipes 1975.

Publication of Elizabeth David's cookery books from the beginning of the 1950s was a symptom of new interests in cookery. Her books have remained a profound influence on British home cooking.

Tiffin

Base: 1lb crushed biscuits (malted milk)	1 tbsp sugar
	2 tbsp syrup.
2 tablespoons drinking chocolate/cocoa	Top: 4ozs cooking chocolate
4ozs margarine	4 tbsp icing sugar.

Method: Melt margarine; syrup, cocoa and sugar in pan. Add biscuits. Set in swiss roll tin in fridge. Melt cooking chocolate, add icing sugar and a little milk if needed to mix to a spreadable butter cream. Spread on base. Leave to set, before cutting into fingers.

Grange Park Women's Institute Recipes 1975.

Chablis Cup

1 bottle Chablis	1 tumbler soda water
1 sherry glass of sherry	any chosen small summer fruits
1pt boiling water	
6 lumps of sugar	8 ice cubes.
1 thin strand of lemon peel	

Method: Dissolve sugar in the boiling water, add lemon peel and leave for 30 minutes. Strain, add Chablis and sherry, chill thoroughly for 30 minutes. Just before service add chosen fruits, soda water and ice cubes, and serve.

NOTE:Skinless segments of sweet orange; thinly sliced unskinned cucumber (which is not a fruit!); peeled, stoned, halved grapes; peeled segments of pear cut like skinned, sliced peaches - with a silver knife, stoned, black or white cherries, and always when available - a sprig of two of the mixed drinks herb - borage.

'Fanny Cradock Invites' 1970.

Carrot Soup with Orange and Tarragon

—— 4 Servings ——

Carrot and orange soup is often spoilt, I feel, by the use of far too much oil to sauté the vegetables initially and adding cream at the end. Neither is necessary. Nor does the soup need much, if any, salt - it will spoil the delicate, rather sweet flavour and light texture. Fresh tarragon is wonderful for this soup, but dried is perfectly all right - it reconstitutes itself quickly in the liquid.

1lb (500g) carrots	$1\frac{1}{2}$ pints (1l) chicken
1 onion	stock
1 medium potato	1 tablespoon fresh
1 orange	chopped tarragon, or 1
6 cardamom pods	teaspoon dried

Roughly chop the carrots, onion and potato. Brush out a heavy saucepan with oil and sauté the vegetables for about 3 minutes.
Meanwhile, grate the peel of the orange, then squeeze its juice and rind, the cardamom, and stock. Bring to a simmer, cover and cook for 25 minutes. Add the tarragon in the last 5 minutes of cooking. Blend very well: the texture should be as smooth as possible. Serve with triangles of wholemeal toast or warmed brown rolls.
'Healthy Food in Half and Hour' Jenny Rogers 1987.

Trout Marinated with Yoghurt and Spices

—— 6 Servings ——

The wise man dismisses nothing.
He stands at the banks of a fast-flowing river.
Not dismayed by the raging torrent that blocks his path.
He wonders where it is going.
And while pondering upon these thoughts, he will sip a glass of lassi.

This iced and salted yoghurt, flavoured with aromatics, will free his mind of concern and liberate the gastric juices and turn his thoughts to the fragrant spices of the orient. Which, my friends, can be yours if you follow these instructions.

6 trout	pepper
$\frac{1}{2}$ teaspoon paprika	1 tablespoon dill
4 tablespoons coriander	$\frac{1}{2}$ green pepper, deseeded
seeds	2 tablespoons freshly
$\frac{1}{2}$ teaspoon salt	chopped mint
6 cardomom seeds	Juice of 1 lemon
2 onions, finely chopped	6oz (175ml) natural
2 cloves garlic	yoghurt
$\frac{1}{4}$ teaspoon ground black	Butter for basting

Instead of trout, you can use whiting or perch, or thick fillets of white fish such as hake or cod.
Place all the other ingredients, except the yoghurt, in your liquidizer (or pestle and mortar). Whizz or grind until you have a paste which you then mix with the natural yoghurt.
Clean the fish and spread the paste over and inside them. Leave to marinate for 1 hour.
Grill over a wood fire or under a preheated grill until crisp and cooked. During the cooking process, you should turn the fish from time to time, and baste with butter and the remainder of the marinade.
As you sip your iced lager and flake the flesh of the fish into freshly baked nan bread, uplifted with a fine lime pickle, you may wonder what the first sentences of this recipe signify. But, as they say in the East, if you have to ask you will never know.
'Floyd on Fish' Keith Floyd 1985.

Stir-Fried Gingered Beef

—— 4 servings ——

2 teaspoons soy sauce
1 tablespoon sherry
1 teaspoon sesame oil
1 teaspoon cornflour
2.5cm (1 inch) piece fresh
    root ginger, grated
grated rind of 1 orange
    and 1 tablespoon juice
400g (14oz) beef olives,
    shredded into strips

1cm ($\frac{1}{2}$ inch) wide
1 tablespoon sunflower oil
125g (4oz) mangetouts
$\frac{1}{2}$ x 230g (8oz) can
    waterchestnuts, drained
    and sliced
orange segments to garnish

Place the soy sauce, sherry, sesame oil, cornflour, ginger, orange rind and juice in a bowl. Stir in the beef and leave to marinate for at least 15 minutes. Remove the beef with a slotted spoon; reserve the marinade.
Heat the sunflower oil in a large frying pan or wok, add the beef and stir-fry for 3-5 minutes, until browned.
Stir in the marinade, mangetouts and waterchestnuts and cook for 5 minutes. Serve immediately, garnished with orange and accompanied by rice noodles. Preparation time: 5 minutes, plus marinating. Cooking time: 8-10 minutes. Freezing: Not recommended.
'Good Fast Food' Clare Gordon-Smith 1986.

Imam Bayildi

You too will faint at the taste of these aubergines! In Turkey imam bayildi are all too often seen floating in a puddle of luke warm grease. Not so our version.

—— 6 Servings ——

3 plump aubergines
1 large onion, chopped
2 courgettes, chopped
1 red and 1 green pepper,
    chopped
2 fat garlic cloves, crushed
4 tablespoons olive oil
2 bay leaves
1 tablespoon marjoram
1 tablespoon basil
$\frac{1}{2}$ tablespoon cumin
$\frac{1}{2}$ tablespoon cardamom

6oz (175g) toasted
    almonds, roughly
    chopped
juice of 1 lemon
8oz (225gm) lexia raisins
7floz (200ml) red wine
$1\frac{1}{2}$lb (700gm) cooked
    rice
1lb (450gm) strong
    cheddar, grated
6 tomatoes, sliced

Halve aubergines lengthwise, and scoop out middles with a soupspoon. Roughly chop the removed flesh.
Saute vegetables and chopped aubergine in oil with bay leaves. When onion softens, add the rest of the herbs and spices, cover, and continue cooking until aubergine is soft. Remove from heat.
Add nuts, lemon juice, fruit, wine, rice and cheese (reserving a little for topping), and mix well. Check seasoning.
Pile mix into aubergine shells,. Decorate with tomato slices and remaining cheese. Bake at 180°C for 1 hour, covered with foil.
'Cooking with Stones' Stones Restaurant, Avebury. Recipe by Hilary Howard 1989.

Redcurrant Flans

—— 6 Servings ——

These delightful little flans are ideal for al fresco summer parties. If fresh redcurrants cannot be found, use canned or frozen ones.

50g (2oz) caster sugar
150ml ($\frac{1}{4}$ pint) rosé wine
500g (1lb) redcurrants

2 tablespoons redcurrant
    jelly
6 individual sponge flan
    cases

Place the sugar and wine in a saucepan and heat gently until dissolved. Add the redcurrants, cover and cook gently for 3 minutes. Remove with a slotted spoon and set aside. Boil the liquid for a few minutes, until reduced and syrupy. Stir in the redcurrant jelly and heat gently until melted.
Divide the redcurrants between the flan cases and brush them with the glaze.
Serve with Greek strained yoghurt or whipped cream.
Variation
Replace the redcurrants with blackcurrants.
Preparation time: 10 minutes
Freezing: Not recommended
'Good Fast Food' Clare Gordon-Smith 1986.

Peach Cake

1.5kg peaches (about 13)
250g sugar
1 lemon
200g butter
4 eggs
300g self-raising flour

100g ground almonds
1 teaspoon ground
aniseeds
grease for baking tray
150g cranberries

Pour boiling water over peaches, skin them, half them and stone them. Bring 50g sugar and 1/4 of litre of water with lemon juice to the boil. Steam peach-halfs in that liquid for about 8 minutes on low heat. Sieve juice off and let peaches cool (sieve off into saucepan). Mix butter, rest of sugar, eggs and grated rind of lemon peel. Mix into smooth dough with flour, almonds and aniseeds. Pour out onto greased baking tray. Put peaches on dough and cranberries on top of peaches and dough. Bake at gas 5/200 c for about 40 minutes. Mix cornflower with little water, bring the juice sieved off earlier to boil and stir in cornflower. Use as glazing on finished cake.
Gill Corbishley.

27

Eating Out

A world in which a large proportion of the population never ate a meal outside their own home seems remote from life as it is in the 1990s. But a hundred years ago restaurants were only available to limited numbers and categories of people. Chop-houses, where a middle-income man could eat his lunch, existed, and there had, of course, been facilities for the rich to eat in hotels and inns for centuries. The poor made do with take-away food from street vendors, eel and pie shops and the occasional sprat supper. The first fish and chip shops were opened around 1870, when it became possible to keep fish frozen and transport it away from the coast.

The coming of the railways meant that Tea Rooms began to be provided, where gentlemen and ladies could eat out. By the turn of the century, both Lyons and the ABC ran chains of tea rooms, while many smaller concerns also sprang up.

"They went out to lunch. The world is divided into those who have lunch in their own homes, those who have lunch in some one else's, those who have lunch in hotel restaurants, those who have lunch in nice eating-shops, those who have lunch in less nice eating-shops, such as A.B.C.'s, those who have lunch in eating-shops very far from nice, those who have lunch in handkerchiefs, and those who do not have lunch at all." 'Non-Combatants and Others' Rose Macaulay 1916.

What the railways had done for tea rooms, the motor-car did for coaching inns. Between the two world wars the Bright Young Things flocked to road-houses to eat and drink. During and immediately after the Second World War restaurants, struggling with their ration 'points', were generally used more from necessity than as a luxury.

But from the late 1950s onwards several things began to happen which brought a dramatic change in the number and variety of restaurants.

First came a flood of refugees from Communist China. By the mid 1960s every medium-sized town in Britain had its Chinese restaurant. They provided excitingly original food cheaply and unpretentiously. The growing student population and the

Thorogood's

12, Station Road,   *Clacton-on-Sea.*

Japanese Tea Rooms.

Norman Jacobs.

teenage workforce with spare money for luxuries could enjoy this new kind of food without having to worry about wearing the right clothes for the restaurant or which knife and fork to use.

Young people also provided the custom for milk bars, coffee bars and cafeterias such as Steak Express and The Golden Egg. Less adventurous family parties were also looking for alternatives to home cooking and these were soon provided by places like the Quality Inn, the Chicken Inn and, after 1965, by Pizza Express, followed by Pizzaland and Pizza Hut. Burger bars, like Wimpy, MacDonalds and

"But the manager of the 'Imperial' was unimpressed by numbers or necessity and manfully upheld the integrity of British hotel-keeping. Tea, he explained, was served daily in the Palm Court, with orchestra on Thursdays and Sundays, between the hours of four and six. A table d'hote dinner was served in the dining-room from seven-thirty until nine o'clock. An a la carte dinner was also served in the grill-room at the same time. It was now twenty minutes past six. If the gentlemen cared to return in an hour and ten minutes he would do his best to accommodate them, but he could not promise to reserve a table. Things were busy that day. There had been motor races in the neighbourhood, he explained."
'Vile Bodies' Evelyn Waugh 1930.

ABOVE: *Thorogood's Japanese Tea Rooms in Clacton, Essex c1903.*

BELOW: *Thorogood's Bakery, Clacton c1903.*

Norman Jacobs.

Burger King, were direct competition for restaurants serving fried chicken or pizzas. By 1992 public distaste for red meat and fatty foods has prompted MacDonalds to diversify: Now they too are selling pizzas.

It is once again people's increasing mobility which is cited as the reason for their interest in foreign food and the enormous popularity of foreign restaurants in Britain since the 1970s. Cheap air travel and foreign holidays have created a demand for a great variety of food and drink in British restaurants.

Soho, in London, has been a home for refugees and ex-patriates from France, Russia, Hungary, Greece and

Italy who have been running restaurants there since the early years of this century. Now they have been joined by Turkish, Mexican, Malaysian, Chinese, African, Lebanese and Indian restauranteurs. In smaller towns the Indian restaurant first followed the pattern set by Chinese immigrants a few years earlier. By employing family members and staying open late the restaurants were able to offer cheap, tasty food when nothing else was available. In the last ten years a far more varied and interesting range of food has been offered in many Chinese and Indian restaurants, as they have become a more up-market option.

An interesting development in restaurants during the 1980s was begun by Paul Bocuse, a French chef. His 'Nouvelle Cuisine' and 'Cuisine Minceur' was both very popular and very expensive. He used only fresh ingredients, presenting small portions of food. On the whole 'nouvelle cuisine' failed to find popularity with a general public who wished, at least, to feel full for their money. Although it no longer seems possible to find a restaurant which still calls what it serves 'nouvelle cuisine', it did serve to encourage a trend towards fresher ingredients and better cooking in some sorts of restaurant.

The only style of restaurant it is rather difficult to find among the thousands which exist at the end of the twentieth century is one which is typically English. It is still possible to find a chop-house, though only the grandest sort, in London and there is still the odd eel and pie shop around, but these are a tiny minority. In 1992 it is the Happy Eater which, together with the Little Chef and Trusthouse Forte, supplies a range of sandwiches, salads, burgers, jacket-potatoes, fried foods and sweets to the traveller, which shows the fastest growth in sales since 1986 (79%). Fast Food is the name given to this sort of catering - its nationality is not specific and its popularity seems limitless.

The Curry Story

Which ever-popular dish can be found in magazines, recipe-books and on radio and television programmes throughout the century? As long ago as 1894 'Home Notes' regularly carried recipes for currying meat, fish and eggs. In 1927 Miss Kate Lovell gave a talk in the series 'Household Talks' on the BBC's wireless service describing the making of a curry by "an old uncle of mine who was an army officer and had been stationed out in India for years." Before the advent of spaghetti bolognaise, many British housewives must have been encouraged by these recipes, or by personal contact with civil servants and army personnel who had lived in the east, to cheer up a mince dish with some curry powder. Apples and sultanas were often added to sweeten the final dish.

But curry is an inadequate name for the subtle and complex recipes such as Shakoothi (Goan-style chicken with roasted coconut) which can now be cooked using recipe books such as Madhur Jaffrey's 'Indian Cookery'. The ubiquitous carton of curry-powder has been replaced in many cooks' cupboards by a range of fresh, frozen and dried whole spices which they use as a recipe requires.

Contact with Indian cookery other than through the British Empire has come in restaurants run by immigrants where it is possible to sample the delights of the Tandoori oven and other exotica and also in everyday contacts with the growing number of Indian residents in Britain.

As the century ends, the range of food offered in Indian restaurants is becoming more varied. At home ready-cooked bhajias are often eaten together with home-made or ready-prepared chicken and lamb dishes. For those who are happy to prepare a curry-sauce and throw in their chosen ingredients the wheel has come full circle: A recipe book is published which reveals the secret of Indian restaurant cookery and tells you how to do just that!

BELOW: A banquet for Nanjit Nawanogar in 1907.

Something to Drink

All sorts of drinks, tea and Horlicks, as well as the wine mentioned by Anthony Powell, became luxury items during the Second World War because of the blockade of shipping and the rationing system.

The story of what people were drinking from 1900 onwards, like the story of food, is one of steady expansion of both volume and diversity of manufactured products which was only briefly interrupted by the world wars. At the beginning of the century poorer people drank tea or home-brewed beer almost exclusively. Barley water and fruit syrups were made at home for invalids and children. For the more well-to-do it was becoming possible to buy commercially produced beer and beverages in ever-greater variety.

The commercial beer trade was encouraged when duties on beer and glass were repealed in the 1830s and by 1880 Whitbread's beer was so popular that the labels carried the request: "when empty please destroy the label". The temptation to re-sell the bottle full of home-brew was obviously widespread!

Jacob Schweppe first sold artificially produced mineral waters in England in the 1790's and firms, such as L Rose & Co, had sold bottled fruit juices, mainly lime and lemon, from the middle of the nineteenth century. 'Fruit cordials' were looked upon as a medical tonic, especially effective in the relief of rheumatism. Lucozade, which was always sold as a health drink which 'aids recovery', was manufactured from similar ingredients, essentially sugar and water, from 1927 onwards. In 1991 Lucozade sales

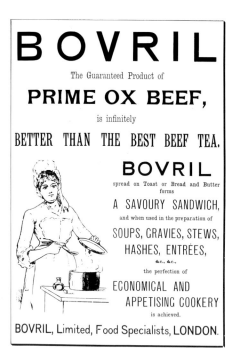

BOVRIL

The Guaranteed Product of

PRIME OX BEEF,

is infinitely

BETTER THAN THE BEST BEEF TEA.

BOVRIL

spread on Toast or Bread and Butter forms

A SAVOURY SANDWICH,

and when used in the preparation of

SOUPS, GRAVIES, STEWS, HASHES, ENTRÉES,

&c., &c.,

the perfection of

ECONOMICAL AND APPETISING COOKERY

is achieved.

BOVRIL, Limited, Food Specialists, LONDON.

exceeded £120 million, a position it owes to the success of Lucozade Sport which claims to be 'isotonic' - feeding water and sugar quickly into the bloodstream after exercise.

Fizzy drinks, kept bubbly by delightful devices such as the Hamilton cap, where the bottle was stored on its side to keep the cork moist, and the Codd, with its marble held tight against the rubber ring by gas pressure, were a rare treat for English children in 1900. Soda-water was originally so named because sodium bicarbonate was used to make it fizzy, but it then became a general title for many highly-flavoured American drinks. Flavours like sarsparilla (an extract from the dried

ABOVE: Hamilton bottle and lemonade bottles.

roots of a Jamaican shrub), orgeat (a mixture of barley or almond extract with orange-flower water) are now almost forgotten. The simpler flavours of orange and lemon dominated the fruit squashes, which were ubiquitous in the 1950s, 60s and 70s.

Changes in drinking habits, for soft drinks at least, followed the 'healthy eating' doctrines of the 1980s.

BELOW: At Langley Moor Working Men's Club, Durham in 1955.

English Heritage

Hulton Deutsch Collection.

Squashes, with their high sugar content and synthetic colourings, became less popular and packaging made pure fruit juice, treated to retain a long-life and with all-natural sugar content, an attractive alternative. Mineral-waters remain as popular as ever and are consumed in ever-greater quantities, although many people prefer to buy 'traditional', cloudy lemonade, ginger-beer with nineteenth-century pictures on the cans and flavours such as dandelion and burdock which give a spurious impression of nutritive value. In the 1990s it is also possible to buy an infinite variety of 'natural', 'healthy' spa waters to which only bubbles, preservatives and a twist of flavouring have been added!

But the most popular fizzy drink in Britain at the end of the twentieth century must be Coca-Cola. It is no longer made from the products of the addictive cola plant. What it is made from is a closely-guarded secret. Factories all over the world, constructed exactly the same, are shipped Coca-Cola ingredients from America in steel drums and make up the drink to be sold in their own country. In the 1880s Coca-Cola was first marketed as a cure for headaches and the distinctively-shaped bottle was introduced in 1915. Cans, which appeared in the 1950s, have almost completely replaced the bottle in this country, although they can still be bought in many other countries. 'Coke' has become more than just a drink: it is also a design icon and cultural statement.

If there is a suspicion that fizzy drinks full of sugar, despite their health claims, are not essential for life, the manufacturers no doubt take comfort from the knowledge that centuries of certainty about the evil effects of alcohol have not discouraged its consumption. Through the twentieth century the British have continued to consume cocktails, which originated in America at the beginning of the nineteenth century and reached their peak of popularity there during the prohibition of liquor from 1919 onwards. Whisky, gin and other spirits are also being sold in larger and larger quantities. More spare money, more spare time and the relatively lower cost of wine and spirits have contributed to

the trend. Wine, which used only to be available from off-licences and pubs, is now easy to pick up with groceries in any supermarket. This, perhaps helped by the taste for wine created during holidays abroad and the good-quality selection now supplied courtesy of the European Community and modern production methods, has created the change.

Benefit to health has always been an advertising claim for the other new sorts of drinks which were appearing at the beginning of this century. Fry, Cadbury and Rowntree all produced cocoa drinks in the second half of the nineteenth century. These were quickly rivalled by Horlicks, which was patented in Chicago in 1883 and produced in Slough in 1906, and Ovaltine from the British Ovaltine Company, which was formed in 1909. A milky drink before retiring to bed was promoted as the ONLY method of ensuring adequate, healthy rest. The continuing presence of all these products on sale demonstrates their appeal to large numbers of people.

Perhaps the story of coffee through the twentieth century is an accurate reflection of the sorts of change which have occurred. At the beginning of the

century only a small number of better-off people drank coffee. Beans were bought, roasted and ground at home on the whole, although Thomas Lipton had already begun to sell packages of ready-ground coffee in his shops. Coffee essence had also been sold since the 1850s, and the arrival of Camp coffee in 1885 eventually made sales higher than those of real coffee. The invention of instant coffee, which was first sold in England in 1939, completely changed the market; Camp was relegated to cake-making and the nation began to drink coffee by the gallon.

The next change, prompted by the move from 'synthetic' to 'real' in people's minds and by the development of vacuum-sealed ground coffee and a variety of efficient kitchen machinery for making coffee at reasonable prices, was a movement back to coffee without additives which began in the 1980s. Today, as with most other things we eat and drink, there is a bewildering range of choice: instant, filter, espresso, percolator, decaffeinated, with chicory, with chocolate (!). Today, it seems, we can consume almost anything, as long as we can afford to buy it.

Celebrations

It is difficult to call to mind any British ceremony or celebration which is not accompanied by food. At all the great occasions in the Christian year; Christmas, Lent, Easter and Harvest, traditional food is eaten. Now that other communities, such as Muslims and Hindus are established in many towns, other traditions, invariably celebrated with food, are also observed. At personal celebrations, like birthdays, christenings, bar mitzvahs, weddings, even funerals, food and drink is almost always provided.

> "Heaped up on the floor, to form a kind of throne, were turkeys, geese, game, poultry, brawn, great joints of meat, sucking pigs, long wreaths of sausages, mince-pies, plum puddings, barrels of oysters, red-hot chestnuts, cherry-cheeked apples, juicy oranges, luscious pears, immense twelfth-cakes, and seething bowls of punch, that made the chamber dim with their delicious steam".
> 'A Christmas Carol' Charles Dickens 1852.

A comparison between the Christmas food described by Charles Dickens in 'A Christmas Carol', written in 1852, and the 'Festive Fare for Christmas' suggested in a Ministry of Food pamphlet in 1945 demonstrates the wide range of possibilities for differences in even that most traditional menu.

Of course the pitiful scarcity of ingredients available during the Second World War was responsible for the austerity of the 1945 menu. But there have undoubtedly been changes and modifications in Christmas and Easter recipes since 1900. 'Middle Class Cookery' by 'Vera', which was published around the turn of the century, suggests that the goose for roasting should be allowed to hang for a few days and lists roast sucking pig, "not more than twenty days old", as one suitable sort of meat among many. 1980s equivalents from a Schwartz spices recipe book are Stuffed Duck with Orange and Cranberry Sauce and

BELOW: Children's party at Battersea Town Hall in January 1928 in the presence of the Duke and Duchess of York (later King George VI and Queen Elizabeth).

32

Loins of Pork with Herby Stuffing. Emphasis has moved away from the selection of good quality meat and its careful cooking to the creation of a meat dish, in which several ingredients combine and enhance the meat.

Christmas puddings and cakes and mince pies are dishes which are recognisably the same in the 1990s as they were in the 1890s. Many of the same recipes are still used, handed down in families or kept alive in cookery books. But these rich, indigestible dried fruit dishes are now almost the sole survivors of dozens of boiled puddings and fruit cakes which were commonly eaten in the eighteenth and nineteenth centuries. We cling to our traditions but most of us prefer sweeter, more digestible fresh fruits or fruit substitutes and chocolate desserts as we enter the twenty-first century. Perhaps Christmas Puddings will be only a memory in another hundred years?

Although Hot Cross Buns show no sign of being forgotten as a traditional Easter dish, an Easter Simnel Cake is seldom made in the 1990s. Chocolate Easter Eggs, on the other hand, belong firmly to the second half of the century. Pancakes are still clung to by many, rolled up with lemon-juice and sugar, for Shrove Tuesday, even in a world where whole restaurants serve nothing but pancakes, savoury and sweet in every conceivable permutation, throughout the year.

A G Street's description of a Harvest Supper in 1906 in 'Farmer's Glory' does not sound very much like the gatherings for cold meats, salads and sweet and savoury flans with which many church communities celebrate harvest in the last years of the twentieth century. He writes:

"The big barn would be cleared out sufficiently to make room for the seating of thirty or forty people. The words 'God Speed the Plough' in letters eighteen inches high, on the wall at one end, would be freshened up with whitewash; this was usually my job. A local caterer would arrive in the morning with tables, benches and provender. The menu consisted of cold meat, beef, mutton, or ham, with hot boiled potatoes for the first course, and hot figgety duff puddings with whole raisins in them for the second. They

ABOVE TOP: Celebration dinner for Jewish refugees in London in 1942.

ABOVE: Mothers' Union tea stall at Great Oakley, Essex in the 1920s.

were boiled all the day in the dairy copper....Most of them drank beer...."

Personal celebrations and ceremonies are, necessarily, more varied in their details. Even so, the most individual of celebrations almost always reflects unconsciously the atmosphere and values of its own time and conveys far more information than the simple details of diet.

33

Finding out more

Topics  Where to start Looking   Official Sources

Topics	Where to start Looking	Official Sources
The Twentieth Century	At home - older relations, photos, scrap-books, reminiscences.	Local museum National museums Archive offices Local history societies
Advertising	Old books & newspapers Junk shops for old catalogues, magazines, cards. Copies of old posters.	Robert Opie Museum
Radio, TV & Cinema	Write to BBC or local television & radio stations	Museum of the Moving Image
Farming and Food production	Local farms, agricultural shows, farming magazines.	Agricultural museums, Ministry of Agriculture, Fisheries and Food
Shopping	Local shops	Museums of social history Supermarket chains - Sainsbury, Marks and Spencer, Gateway etc
Kitchens and Kitchen Utensils	At home Ask relatives Magazines	Historic houses Museums Shops
Eating In	Recipe books, novels.	Library
Eating Out	Local restaurants, novels, food columns of newspapers.	Library
Recipes	Second-hand book shops, magazines, TV.	

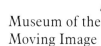

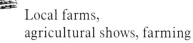
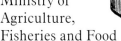

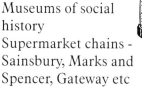

Bibliography

Cookery Books

Allison, Sonia, 'The Dairy Book of Home Cookery' Wolfe Publishing 1968.

Board of Education, 'Food From Overseas Recipes: Food Education Memo No 4', HMSO 1941.

Bocuse, Paul, 'The New Cuisine' Granada Publishing 1978. ISBN 0-246-10983-1.

Cantor, David and Kay & Swann, Daphne, 'The Cranks Recipe Book' J M Dent 1982. ISBN 0-586-06090-1.

Cradock, Fanny and Johnnie, 'Fanny Cradock Invites' BBC Publications 1970. ISBN 0-563-09374-9.

Daily Express, 'Prize Recipes for Fish Cookery' The Lane Publications, Undated c1925.

David, Elizabeth, 'French Country Cooking' Penguin 1959 (first published 1951). ISBN 0-14-046789-0.

Dhillon, Kris, 'The Curry Secret: Indian Restaurant Cooking at Home' Paperfronts 1989. ISBN 0-7160-0809-2.

Evans, Gill, 'Schwartz Cooking with Herbs and Spices' Schwartz Spices Undated c1980.

Floyd, Keith, 'Floyd On Fish' BBC Publications 1985. ISBN 0-563-20422-2.

FitzGibbon, Theodora, 'A Taste of the West Country' Pan 1975. ISBN 0-330-24364-0.

FitzGibbon, Theodora, 'A Taste of London' Pan 1976. ISBN 0-330-24580-5.

Gordon-Smith, Clare, 'Good Fast Food' J Sainsbury/Woodhead-Faulkner 1986.

Harben, Philip, 'Cooking With Harben' Herbert Jenkins 1953.

Howard, Hilary and Stapleton, Julia, 'Cooking With Stones' Stones Print 1989. ISBN 0-9514076-0-0.

Jaffrey, Madhur, 'Indian Cookery' BBC Publications 1982. ISBN 0-563-16491-3.

Lindsay, Jessie and Mottram, V M, 'Manual of Modern Cookery' University of London Press 1927.

Rogers, Jenny, 'Healthy Food in Half an Hour' Penguin 1987. ISBN 0-14-046809-9.

Richmond, Lillie, 'Domestic and Economical Cookery Recipes' Cartwright and Rattray 1892.

Singh, Dharamjit, 'Indian Cookery' Penguin 1970. ISBN 0-14-046-141-8.

Skinner, Zena, 'Town and Around Recipes' BBC Publicatons 1965.

Smith, Delia, 'The Evening Standard Cook Book' Coronet Books 1978. ISBN 0-340-23094-0.

Stone, Marie, 'The Covent Garden Cookbook' Allison and Busby 1974. ISBN 0-85031-146-2.

Turner, Joe, 'The Sainsbury Book of Cocktails and Party Drinks' Cathay Books 1982. ISBN 0-86178-182-1.

Vera, 'Middle-Class Cookery' R S Cartwright Undated c1900.

White, Florence, 'Good Things in England' Jonathan Cape 1932.

Contemporary Sources

Adburgham, Alison, 'Yesterday's Shopping: Army & Navy Stores Mail Order Catalogue 1907' David and Charles 1969. ISBN 0-7153-4692-X.

'British Workman and Home Monthly Annual' S W Partridge & Co. 1907.

Carlton, Paul, 'Simple Vegetarian Cooking' Harrap 1931.

'Home, Health and Garden' BBC Publications 1928.

Fisher Barham, 'Yesterday and Today around Falmouth and Penryn' Glasney Press 1981. ISBN 09063540-4-8.

Garth, Margaret and Wrench, Stanley, 'Home Management' Daily Express Publications 1934.

'Girls' Own Annual', 1899.

'The Geographical Magazine' Chatto and Windus March 1947.

'Household Encyclopedia' Harmsworth 1923.

Isobel, 'Home Notes' C Arthur Pearson Volume 1 January-April 1894.

Jacobs, Norman, 'The Sunshine Coast' Tyndale and Panda Publishing 1986. ISBN 1-870094-03-4. Contemporary photographs from Clacton and other coastal resorts.

Spargo, Demelza (Ed), 'This Land is Our Land: Aspects of Agriculture in English Art' Royal Agricultural Society of England 1989. ISBN 0-9513854-0-2. Exhibition catalogue.

'The Smallholder Magazine' 1913-1914.

Ward, Harold, 'Herbal Manual' C W Daniel & Co. 1934.

Reference and Social History

Adburgham, Alison, 'Shops and Shopping 1800-1914' Barrie and Jenkins 1989. ISBN 0-7126-2114-8.

Atkinson, Frank, 'Pictures from the Past: Northern Life' Collins and Brown 1991. ISBN 1-85585-067-2.

Beck, Doreen, 'The Book of Bottle Collecting' Hamlyn 1973. ISBN 0-600-34-716-8.

Briggs, Asa, 'A Social History of England' Weidenfeld and Nicolson 1983. ISBN 0-297-78074-3.

Brydson, John, 'Plastics' Her Majesty's Stationery Office 1991. ISBN 0-11-290478-5.

Boniface, Priscilla, 'Hotels and Restaurants 1830 to the present day' Royal Commission on the Historical Monuments of England 1981. ISBN 0-11-700993-8.

Black, Maggie, 'Food and Cooking in Nineteenth Century Britain' English Heritage 1985. ISBN 1-85074-085-2.

Coates, Doris, 'Tuppenny Rice and Treacle: Cottage Housekeeping 1900-1920' David and Charles 1975. ISBN 0-7153-7060-X.

Corbishley, Gill, 'Ration Book Recipes: Some Food Facts 1939-1954' English Heritage 1990. ISBN 1-85074-288-X.

Davidson, Caroline, 'A Woman's Work is Never Done' Chatto and Windus 1982. ISBN 0-7011-3982-X.

Emmerson, Robin, 'Table Settings' Shire Publications 1991. ISBN 0-7478-0139-8.

Eveleigh, David, 'Old Cooking Utensils' Shire Publications 1986. ISBN 0-85263-812-4.

Forty, Adrian, 'Objects of Desire': Design and Society 1750-1980' Thames and Hudson 1986. ISBN 0-500-27412-6.

Fowler, Peter, 'Farms in England' Royal Commission on the Historical Monuments of England 1983. ISBN 0-11-701130-4.

Holley, Erica, 'Food' Dryad Press 1985. ISBN 0-8521-9640-7. Exploring the historical evidence for food in Britain from prehistory to the twentieth century for 14-17 year olds.

Hudson, Kenneth, 'Food, Clothes and Shelter: Twentieth Century Industrial Archaeology' John Baker 1978. ISBN 0-212-97021-6.

Ingram, Arthur, 'Dairying Bygones' Shire Publications 1977. ISBN 0-85263-866-3.

'J S 100: The Story of Sainsbury's' J Sainsbury 1969.

Kitchen, Penny (Comp), 'For Home and Country: Women's Institute Magazines 1919-1959' Ebury Press 1990. ISBN 0-85223-855-X.

Mayhew, Henry, 'London Labour and the London Poor'. 1851.

Montgomery-Massingberd, Hugh and Watkin, David, 'The London Ritz' Aurum Press 1980. ISBN 0-948149-71-X.

Opie, Robert, 'The Art of the Label' Simon and Schuster 1987. ISBN 0-671-65441-1.

Platts, John, 'Living Together: Twentieth Century' Macmillan Educational 1977. ISBN 0-333-15610-2. History project book.

Plimmer, Violet G, 'Food Values in Wartime' Longmans and Green 1941.

Powers, Alan, 'Shopfronts' Chatto and Windus 1989. ISBN 0-7011-3368-6.

Swinglehurst, Edmund, 'The Country Life Book of Britain Then and Now' Octopus 1988. ISBN 1-871307-40-6.

Slaughter, Basil, 'Let's Git Up Agin The Table' Essex Federation of the Workers' Educational Association 1992. ISBN 0-9519265-0-0.

Turnbull, Les and Womack, Simon, 'Home Sweet Home' Gateshead Metropolitan Borough Council 1977. ISBN 0-905977-02-5. Housing in the north east from 1800 to 1977.

Turnbull, Les, 'Discovery Your Neighbourhood' Gateshead Metropolitan Borough Council c1977. An introduction to local studies.

Tannahill, Reay, 'Food in History' Penguin 1988. ISBN 0-1401-0206-X.

Walter Marc, 'Grand Hotel: The Golden Age of Palace Hotels' J M Dent 1984. ISBN 0-160-04667-5.

Fiction and autobiography

Amis, Kingsley, 'Lucky Jim' Gollancz 1954. ISBN 0-575-03484-X.

Ashford, Daisy, 'The Young Visiters' Chatto and Windus 1919.

Byatt, A S, 'The Virgin in the Garden' Penguin 1981 (first published 1978). ISBN 0-14-01-1685-9.

Dickens, Charles, 'A Christmas Carol' 1852.

Hughes, M V, 'A London Home in the 1890's Oxford University Press 1946. ISBN 0-19-281257-2.

Lee, Laurie, 'Cider with Rosie' Penguin 1962. ISBN 0-1400-1682-1.

Macaulay, Rose, 'Non-Combatants and Others' Methuen 1986. ISBN 0-413-60230-3.

Powell, Anthony, 'The Soldier's Art' Collins 1966. Available as a Fontana paperback. ISBN 0-00-654049-X.

Powell, Margaret, 'Below Stairs' Pan 1970. ISBN 0-330-02503-1.

Street, A G, 'Farmer's Glory' Penguin 1951. ISBN 0-14-000837-3.

Thompson, Flora, 'Lark Rise to Candleford' Penguin 1973. ISBN 0-14-09-3672-5.

Waugh, Evelyn, 'Vile Bodies' Penguin 1938 (first published 1930).

Wells, H G, 'The History of Mr Polly' 1910.

Acknowledgements

The author and English Heritage gratefully acknowledge the help given by Ann Hoskyns, Jennifer Ling, Margaret Turnbull, Joan Page, Jenny Pile, Peggy Lord, Norman Jacobs, Treve Rosoman and Robin Wyatt. Permission to reproduce extracts from published work and recipes has kindly been given by:

Peters, Fraser and Dunlop Group (for 'Vile Bodies' and 'Non-Combatants and Others), Random House UK (for 'Cider with Rosie' published by the Hogarth Press), William Heinemann (for 'The Soldier's Art'), Delia Smith (for 'French Onion Soup' and 'Petits Pois à la Française' first published in 1974), Penguin Books (for 'Carrot Soup with Orange and Tarragon' and 'The Virgin in the Garden'), Reed International Books (for 'Bucks Fizz'), Martin Books (for 'Redcurrant Flans' and 'Stir-Fried Gingered Beef'), BBC Enterprises (for 'Trout Marinated with Yoghurt and Spices', 'Shellfish and Grapefruit Salad' and 'Chablis Cup') and Stones Restaurant (for 'Imam Bayildi').

We have made every effort to find the owners of the copyright of material in this book and apologise to any we have not located.

RIGHT: *Hull fishing industry, February 1951.*

BACK COVER: *Cast iron ranges from the George Wright & Co. catalogue 1905.*